THE
LEATHERCRAFT
BOOK

THE LEATHERCRAFT BOOK

PAT HILLS

WITH JOAN WIENER

Random House New York

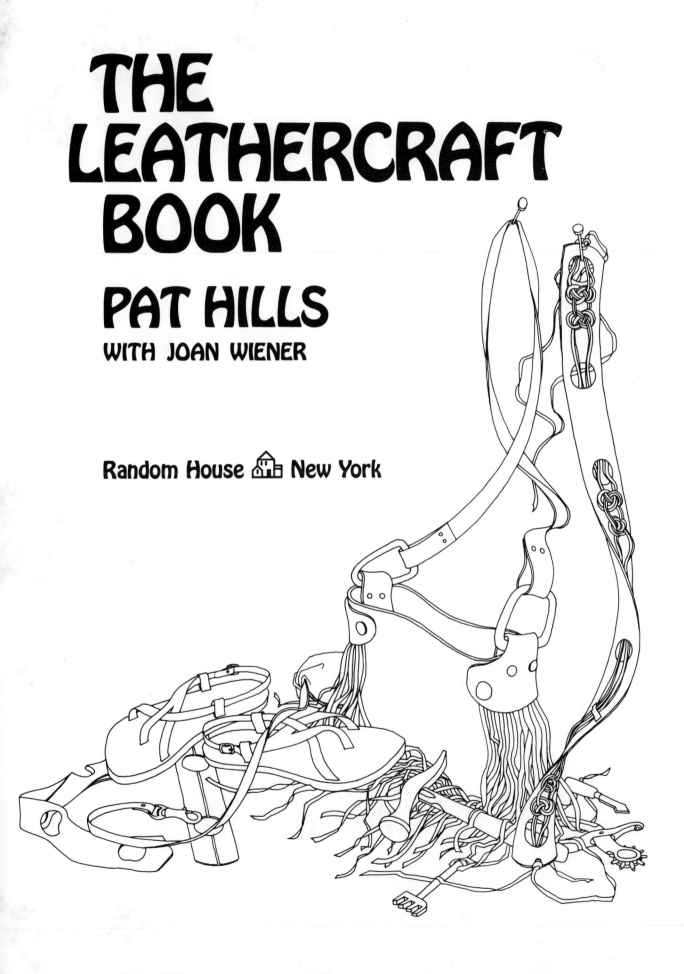

ISBN: 0-394-47416-3 (hardbound)
ISBN: 0-394-70621-8 (paperbound)

Manufactured in the United States of America

First Edition

Illustrations by Pat Hills
Title page and section title drawings by Howard Burns
Design by J. K. Lambert

CONTENTS

INTRODUCTION TO LEATHERCRAFT 1

LEATHER 3

TOOLS AND SUPPLIES 9

TECHNIQUES IN LEATHERCRAFT 23

PROJECTS   47

DIRECTORY OF SUPPLIERS   127

THE LEATHERCRAFT BOOK

INTRODUCTION

On a trip to Patagonia, Charles Darwin saw leather being used in a
very primitive way. These Stone Age people would sling animal skins
over their shoulders on the windward side. As the wind changed
direction, they would switch the skins to meet it.

The use of leather predates written history, and it must not have
taken too long for our ancestors to realize that in addition to its
usefulness, leather is a beautiful material to behold.

This book tells you how to use leather to make beautiful and useful
things for yourself—*easily*. It gives simple patterns for belts, handbags
and sandals, as well as some plain general advice on making leather
garments.

At the beginning of the book you will find information on buying
leather and supplies, on the use of tools, and on the techniques of the
craft.

Every pattern has, at the top, a label that will tell you whether it is
"easy," "intermediate" or "advanced." Start with easy things—a plain,
handsome belt, perhaps—and in a very short time you will have learned
enough to make some of the more intricate designs. More important,
once you learn the techniques, you'll be able to design your own
projects without any difficulty.

Leather and leathercraft tools are available throughout the country,
either in shops or by mail order. A very brief list of dealers is included
at the back of the book, but there probably are other suppliers in your

locality. Read the material in the book on doing business with leather suppliers, and make friends with your local dealer—it will be the beginning of a very happy relationship.

Working with leather is easy. It saves you a lot of money. It is quick, it is fun to do. You are lucky to be getting started.

LEATHER

Where to Buy Your Leather

The way to start on leathercraft is to buy the leather. Leather is available, tanned and processed, in leather stores, craft shops, shoe-supply companies, department stores, fabric stores and through mail-order houses and wholesalers.

You can find your own local dealers in the classified section of your local phone book under "Leather Findings" or "Leather."

I recently was browsing through a very fashionable New York department store. The fabrics department had a selection of skins at prices far exceeding those of unchic leather dealers. "Of course," noted the salesman, "we offer you quality." Our skins have no imperfections and are even all the way through."

You are offered this choice, then. As leathercraft increases in popularity, more and more department and fabric stores are going to be carrying hides, kips and skins. Their quality will probably be good, and the shopping convenience even better. Nevertheless, we recommend, whenever possible, that you visit a leather dealer or wholesaler if only for the experience of a vista of floor-to-ceiling skins of every possible color and texture at low prices. A list of dealers is assembled at the back of the book. Try to visit them or other dealers near you when you are in the market for leather.

Types of Leather

Before your first visit to a leather dealer, become familiar with the different types of leather listed here so that you won't panic when you are confronted by what looks like a million rolls.

Animal skins are classified according to size. You will need different size skins and therefore different thickness skins for various projects.

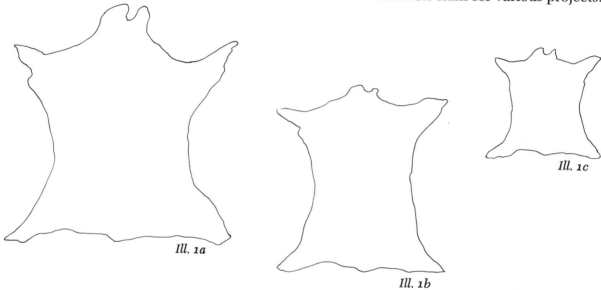

Ill. 1a

Ill. 1b

Ill. 1c

A **hide** (*Ill. 1a*) is the skin of a large animal, such as a steer, cow, bull or horse. Most of what are called hides at your dealer's are actually only half a hide, cut down the center for easier handling during the tanning process. (*Ill. 2*) While hides are available, but since they are usually very heavy, they are best suitable for outside garments and projects calling for heavy-duty leathers.

A **kip** (*Ill. 1b*) is the skin of a large calf or an undersized steer. This leather is usually softer than that of a hide.

The term **skin** (*Ill. 1c*) refers to leather from smaller animals like sheep, lambs, goats and small calves.

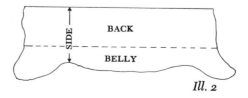

Ill. 2

Cuts of Leather and Their Uses

Hides, kips and skins are usually split by tanners into several layers, just as you might pull pieces of paper off a pad. Each of these layers has a name: Top Grain, Deep Buff, Split and Slab. Hides are split as in illustration 3; skins are smaller and thinner, so are split in fewer layers. (Leather for the soles of shoes, sole leather, is usually not split because the thickness is needed for wear.)

```
                    OUTSIDE
                   TOP GRAIN
                   DEEP BUFF
                     SPLIT
                     SLAB
                    INSIDE          Ill. 3
```

The **Top Grain,** which may also be called Full Grain or Full Top Grain, is the outermost part of the animal. It can come from cattle, horses or pigs, and should be used where strength and durability are important in a project. Top Grain is excellent for belts, bags, sandal straps and soles, bookbinding, upholstery, fancy leather goods, and almost anything you can think of, including fine garments. If you are going to get involved in "tooling,"[1] buy Top Grain but make sure it is vegetable-tanned and not doctored in any way.

Top Grain from kips makes good moccasins, snug-fitting sandal tops, and big floppy shoulder bags. The Top Grain of goats, kids, sheep and lambs, capeskins (South African hair sheep) and cabrettas (Brazilian sheepskins) are all good for making garments.

Chrome Calf, another Top Grain leather, is smooth and lightweight and makes good linings, belts and especially shoe tops.

Latigo Leather is cattle hide tanned with alum and gambier. It is sturdy but soft and pliable and makes great large, rugged carryalls. It comes either in a bright yellow which can be painted, carved,

---

[1] Tooling is the process of decorating your leather by pressing damp leather to create raised and depressed areas.

stained, or stamped, or in a dark brown called "Indian Tanned," which is usually left as is because of its attractive color.

Deep Buff and **Split,** the two middle layers, are much alike. These cuts have no grainy texture and are less strong than the top grain. They are regularly processed to make them look nicer than in their natural state. Deep Buff and Split can be purchased lacquered or with an embossed finish, or roughened or sueded on both sides. (As a matter of fact, the Federal Trade Commission has ruled that these cuts cannot be called "genuine leather.") When Splits are sueded they make nice garments and handbags, or they can be used for backing projects. Most suede jeans are made from Splits.

A Sheep Split is called a *Skiver*. It is used for linings.

Chamois is the under-Split of sheepskin and is good for garments.

The last layer, the **Slab,** is the cut closest to the body of the animal. When it has gone through a process known as sueding, on one side only, it becomes a fine material used for garments, which is correctly called suede. If used for fine handbags, this suede needs to be backed or lined because it is so soft.

Other novelty leathers include *snakeskin,* which makes belts but is paper-thin and requires backing; *lizard* for sandal tops, bags and belts, *ostrich* for the same uses, and even *kangaroo* or *peccary.*

Of course, small skins from young or small animals are so thin that they are not layered. These skins are treated as suede or what is called *kid.* (Kid is properly used only for the skin of a young goat, but the term commonly describes small whole skins.) Small skins are used for projects like belts and garments.

Choosing Your Leather

Let us assume that a beginner in leathercraft will start with basic belt No. 1, the easiest object to make in this book.

How do you buy the suede called for in that belt? First of all, don't be afraid to go into the leather store and ask questions. The owners of these establishments are very anxious that you get started in the craft for which they supply the material, and they are very eager to help you.

Though you can buy leather scraps, a small suede skin will cost in the range of three to five dollars. It would be best to buy such a skin, from which you can easily make three or four belts.

Grades of Leather

Suedes come dyed in a rich variety of colors and in a rich variety of grades. The price varies with the size and the visual quality of the skin. There is no uniform grading in the leather industry. Just examine the skin carefully. Your dealer will help you make your selection, and you will see that leather is graded at the tanner's for surface effects, like holes, uniformity of color, strength and thickness. Because each tanner has his own scale for grading, leather grades vary from one tanner to the next. However, as a general rule, the higher the grade, the fewer the holes or spots.

Weights and Measurements of Leather

When buying leather you should understand its weight and measurements. Most leather is sold by the square foot and the number of square feet in a piece is marked on its reverse side. There will be two numbers: a large number indicating the number of square feet, and a smaller, elevated number indicating the remaining fraction. The smaller number will either be 1, 2 or 3, meaning one-quarter square foot, one-half square foot, or three-quarters square foot. For example, if the back of a piece of leather says 5^1, you know it means 5¼ square feet; 5^2 means 5½ square feet, etc.

Hides run anywhere from 20 to 28 square feet in size. Skins average 6 to 8 square feet, and kips come in between those two.

Ounces: the thickness of leather is described by the ounce; 1/64 of an inch is equal to one ounce. Generally, you only need to think about the weight of your leather in terms of the exact number of ounces when you're worrying about a heavy belt or sandal straps or a very sturdy handbag. Then it's useful to know that hides run from 2 ounces to 10 ounces in thickness and to judge accordingly. In kips and skins, the weight has little relevance. You can judge by eye whether the skin is suitable for your project.

$$2 \text{ oz.} = 1/32 \text{ of an inch thick}$$
$$3 \text{ oz.} = 3/64 \text{ ”   ”   ”   ”}$$
$$4 \text{ oz.} = 1/16 \text{ ”   ”   ”   ”}$$
$$5 \text{ oz.} = 5/64 \text{ ”   ”   ”   ”}$$
$$6 \text{ oz.} = 3/32 \text{ ”   ”   ”   ”}$$
$$7 \text{ oz.} = 7/64 \text{ ”   ”   ”   ”}$$
$$8 \text{ oz.} = 1/8 \text{ ”   ”   ”   ”}$$
$$9 \text{ oz.} = 9/64 \text{ ”   ”   ”   ”}$$
$$10 \text{ oz.} = 5/32 \text{ ”   ”   ”   ”}$$

Irons refer to the thickness of sole leather. Unlike hides, kips and skins, sole leather is sold by the pound. One iron equals 1/48 of an inch thick. When buying leather for sandal soles, you may have to combine irons and ounces. For example, the top sole might be 10 oz. Top Grain flexible belting, while the bottom of the shoe would be prime flexible soling that is 11 irons thick.

TOOLS AND SUPPLIES

The following is a fairly comprehensive list of tools and supplies used in leathercraft. Don't for a moment think that you have to run out and buy all of them. This will leave you frenzied, broke and overloaded. Instead, get the tools you need as you go along. We've put an asterisk in our list before those tools which are more basic than others. These tools can be purchased at leather dealers, wholesalers, shoe-supply companies and, in some instances, art and hardware stores.

You will note that each project in this book begins with a list of tools. In some cases, certain tools can stand in for others. If you just plan to make garments out of lightweight suede, the only tools you'll need are a good sharp pair of scissors and a leather needle.

Measuring and Cutting Tools

Once you've chosen your pattern, leathercraft involves, first of all, measuring and cutting. For cutting you need knives or shears. All of the knives listed below can be bought for under two dollars, either at hardware, art or craft stores or wholesalers who supply shoe-repair shops. The knives I use most are the utility knives and the skife knife, and these are probably what you ought to begin with.

Treat your knives with respect. They cut leather and also human skin. If you're drawing a knife toward you, get out of its way and watch your fingers. *Keep knives out of reach of small children.*

Keep your knives sharp. A dull blade is time-consuming to use, and it makes for stringy edges.

***Utility Knife.** An all-purpose cutting knife that I like best because it can be used for all sorts of projects, except those involving soft leathers like suede. It can be purchased at your local hardware, art or craft store, and it costs less than two dollars. (*Ill. 1*)

Bevel Point Knife. Though this knife is used by many people, it needs resharpening on an oiled stone, a time-consuming process. The utility knife is sturdier and I prefer it to this one. (*Ill. 2*)

Cobbler's Knife. This knife is used by shoemakers for cutting and trimming soles, but unless your hands are very, very strong, it is difficult to use. (*Ill. 3*)

***Skife Knife.** Used to thin—or skive—leather. Because it uses replaceable injection blades, the skife knife needs no sharpening. It is designed so that you can't gouge the leather by cutting too deeply. (*Ill. 4*)

Exacto Knife. A small lightweight knife, excellent for small cutouts. (*Ill. 5*)

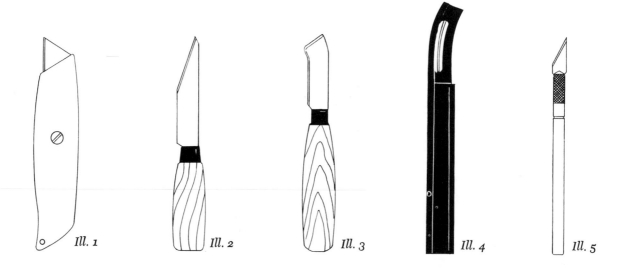

Ill. 1   *Ill. 2*   *Ill. 3*   *Ill. 4*   *Ill. 5*

*Shears. You use shears only for lightweight leathers and suedes. You can buy special leather shears, but any good sturdy pair of scissors will suffice. (*Ill. 6*)

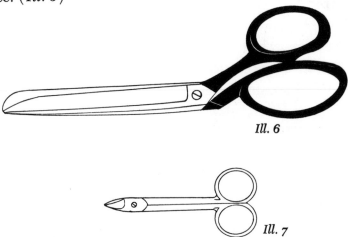

Ill. 6

Ill. 7

Bezel Shears. Though these sturdy shears are sold for metal cutting, they are nice for cutting out small pieces of leather used in appliqué work. They are available in straight and curved blades; I prefer the curved blades for cutting out small petals or other decorations. (*Ill. 7*)

Draw-gauge. This is a useful, but not necessary, tool for cutting straps and belting. It is adjustable. If you invest in one, make sure it is a sturdy metal one. (*Ill. 8*)

Ill. 8

Ill. 9

*Metal Square. A ruler-like guide that is used for almost all your cutting work with the utility knife. It can be used to measure, too. (*Ill. 9*)

*Ruler.** You can use your own metal yardstick or a 12-inch ruler with a metal edge to measure your work.

Cutting Board. Though this isn't a knife or a measuring tool, you need it to do all your leather cutting. Buy a plywood board—I use one 18″ x 33″. Cover your board with a regular artist's matboard in double thickness. This saves the cutting edge of the knife. When the matboard gets too scratched up, simply replace it.

Punches and Affiliated Tools

Punches are used to make holes for stitching in heavy leather. They are also used to make holes for fasteners and buckles, and for slots and holes for sandal straps. Prong and drive punches are used with a hammer, and you should keep your hands out of the way as you punch. Work on an endgrain block or a hardwood stump. The rotary punch is used by hand, plier style.

Though there are punches on the market that cost thirty or forty dollars, most punches are under two dollars and can be purchased at the same sorts of stores in which knives are available.

*Awl or Scribe.** A regular household awl, though it is not technically a punch, can be used to mark a guideline in your leather or suede. (*Ill. 10*)

Ill. 10

*Four-prong Stitching Punch.** This punch, which looks like a fork, is the most widely used. It makes uniformly spaced holes for stitching through heavy leather. (*Ill. 11*)

Five-prong Stitching Punch. A very fine punch for making holes to hand-stitch fine, lightweight leather. It has less spacing between holes than the four-prong punch. (*Ill. 12*)

Slanted-prong Stitching Punch. This punch makes a line of angled holes, commonly used for lacing. (*Ill. 13*)

*One-prong Stitching Punch. This is used for punching single holes on heavy leather. You need it when you are making holes on a curve. (*Ill. 14*)

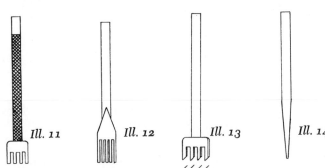

Ill. 11   Ill. 12   Ill. 13   Ill. 14

*Rotary Punch. This tool is a must. It is used primarily to make holes for fasteners and for belt buckles and tongues. It contains six sharp hollow tubes of varying sizes. (*Ill. 15*)

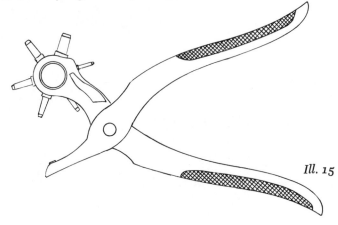

Ill. 15

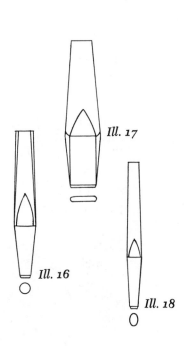

Ill. 17

Ill. 16

Ill. 18

*Drive Punch—round. Used for punching round holes in sandal soles for straps and thongs and also for placing grommets. Different size drive punches are available, but 5/16″ is a nice size for sandals. (*Ill. 16*)

*Drive punch—oblong. Used to make oblong holes in sole leather for sandal straps, as well as holes for attaching buckles. It comes in different sizes, but we recommend 5/8″ for general use. (*Ill. 17*)

Drive punch—oval. Used to make oval holes. The popular sizes are 1/8 to 3/8″. (*Ill. 18*)

*Divider. A compass-like tool which marks a guideline in the leather to show where the stitching punch is used. (*Ill. 19*)

Space Marker. Used to mark holes in a curved line on your leather. Get one to match the spacing of your stitching punch. (*Ill. 20*)

*Rawhide Mallet. This mallet is comfortable to handle and it is used to hit the prong punches through your leather and to tap down glued seams. However, the rawhide mallet is not heavy enough to use with a drive punch through thick leather. (*Ill. 21*)

Rawhide Maul. This cylinder-shaped maul is used with drive punches. It is fast but tiring if you use it for a long job. Hit on the rawhide anyplace on the cylinder. This maul has a metal center and it comes in weights from 2 1/4 to 7 1/2 pounds. The lighter one is suggested for lighter people. (*Ill. 22*)

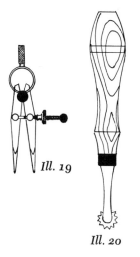

Ill. 19

Ill. 20

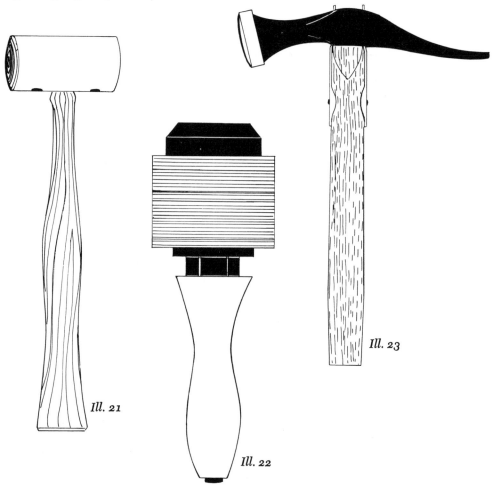

Ill. 21

Ill. 22

Ill. 23

*Metal Hammer. Used primarily for hammering sandal soles together after they are glued. It has a round face so that it won't mark your leather. (*Ill. 23*)

Wood Stump. Though you can buy an endgrain block, you will find that it is expensive. I use a table-height hardwood stump for punching through leather. *Don't* punch on your cutting board or on metal. (*Ill. 24*)

Ill. 24

Stitching Tools

After the stitching holes are punched in your leather with one or several of the prong punches, you are ready to sew or lace your pieces of leather. These evenly spaced holes give you a professional-looking stitch. It is only with lightweight leather that you do not need to pre-punch holes for stitching.

Harness Needle.   This is the most useful of the stitching tools. It is a very sturdy needle with an egg-shaped eye and a dull point. It is used for stitching with waxed thread through pre-punched holes. You would not use it for lightweight suede. It is available in a number of sizes but we recommend No. 000, approximately 2 1/2″ long. Because the harness needle is most often used in pairs, it is good to purchase two. (*Ill. 25*)

Ill. 25 *Ill. 26* *Ill. 27*

Glover's Needle. This needle with a three-cornered point is used on lightweight leather without pre-punching. (*Ill. 26*)

Two-prong Lacing Needle. This needle has a pronged top into which you can slip your lacing without doubling it. (*Ill. 27*)

Pliers. Commonly called lacing pliers, these are used to assist you with lacing as well as with pulling straps through sandals. If you have a household pair with a ridged grip, they will be just fine. (*Ill. 28*)

Lock-stitch Sewing Awl. This tool gives the same effect as a lock stitch on a sewing machine. It is used on heavy leather. (*Ill. 29*)

Sewing Machine. Use your machine to sew lightweight leathers (*page 34*). Set it at a fairly long stitch and test before you begin. My machine has a special gear for leatherwork, and you might check with your own dealer to find out what your machine's capabilities are. It's possible to use the machine without thread to make holes in lightweight leather for stitching. (*Ill. 30*)

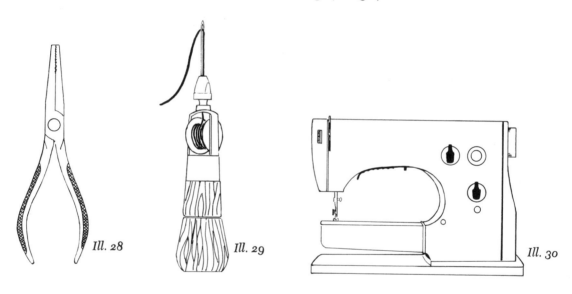

Ill. 28   *Ill. 29*   *Ill. 30*

Ruffing, Grooving and Edging Tools

To give your leatherwork a professional, finished look, it is necessary to smooth out bulky folds and creases and to bevel and burnish edges. As you see, not many of the tools are marked with asterisks. You can improvise replacements, but don't ignore the processes. These tools are inexpensive, however, and do help to make the jobs easy.

*Ruffer. A ruffer is used primarily on smooth leather whose surface is too slick to glue properly. The tool is used to give a rough surface which the glue can penetrate. (*Ill. 31*)

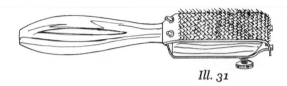

Ill. 31

Adjustable Groover . Used for cutting U-shaped grooves in heavy leather. (*Ill. 32*)

Adjustable V-Gouge. This tool is good for scoring heavy leather in foldlines. It cuts a V-shape, smaller than the groover makes. (*Ill. 33*)

V-Edge Beveler. Used to bevel the edges in leather, for a softer finish. (*Ill. 34*)

Common Edger. Like a V-edge beveler, but for a bigger edge. (*Ill. 35*)

Edge Creaser. This tool makes a groove in the edges of leather. It is a finishing tool, and one you can do without .(*Ill. 36*)

*Hardwood Wheel. (Also called a slick.) This tool burnishes the edge of your leather, giving it a fine finish. (*Ill. 37*)

Ill. 32

Ill. 33

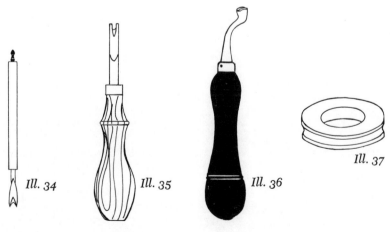

Ill. 34   *Ill. 35*   *Ill. 36*   *Ill. 37*

Special Job Tools

Snap Setter. This is the most inexpensive and convenient tool for putting in snaps. It is used with a hammer. (*Ill. 38*)

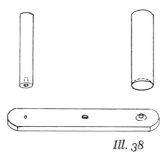

Ill. 38

Grommet Setter. A two-part tool (consisting of a tube and a base with a hole) that comes in about five sizes. The No. oo is the most commonly used. (*Ill. 39*)

Eyelet Setter. A tool that costs less than a dollar and is usually used to make small eyelet fastenings for vest fronts or belts. (*Ill. 40*)

Stud Setter. This handy setter does a number of jobs. It has adapters that enable it to set studs, nailheads, stars and even rhinestones. It has a grommet setter but a one-sided one, which is not as sturdy as the grommet setter mentioned above. (*Ill. 41*)

Ill. 39

Ill. 40

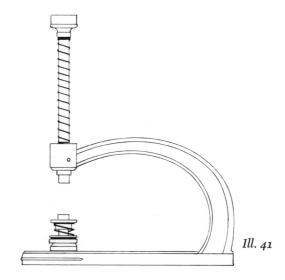

Ill. 41

Landis Sole Cutter. If you buy this wonderful tool new, it will cost you quite a lot of money. I got mine used, for about twenty-five dollars, and you could chip in with a friend or two to get one. It cuts heavy leather like butter and also skives the leather. Replacement blades are available for this super timesaver. (*Ill. 42*)

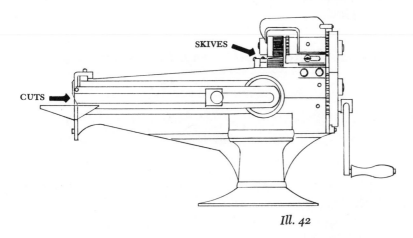

Ill. 42

Motor Drill. The motor is used to sand and wax the edges of sandals and firm leather belts and bags. If you find you are making more than a pair or two of sandals, it is a super timesaver. The motor should be

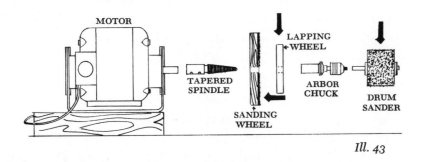

Ill. 43

1/4 horsepower, and does not have to be new. It can come from an old washing machine, as mine did. Mount it firmly in place. Two useful attachments are the tapered spindle and the arbor chuck, seen in the illustration. The tapered spindle or arbor chuck should extend over the edge of the bench or table. This gives you room to manipulate the sandal. The tapered spindle is the least expensive way to get started. The chuck is good, as you can add a drum sander for curved edges. (*Ill. 43*)

Other Supplies

*Waxed Thread.** Good for all hand-stitching, waxed thread is available in natural, black and sometimes brown. These threads are available in several thicknesses. The most commonly used with pre-punched holes is five-cord thread.

Polyester and Heavy-Duty Cotton Thread. For sewing leather on a machine.

* **Rubber Cement.** Office-supply rubber cement is good for hemming garments, as you can pull your hem apart if you have to redo it. It is best bought in a quart container with a brush applicator. For all other jobs, shoe-supply rubber cement is best. It is also bought by the quart and it is available at craft stores and shoemaker suppliers. Buy yourself some cement thinner while you're at it, since someone is bound to leave the top off your glue and produce a thick mess. You can also use the thinner to take excess glue off suede.

*Rivets.** Rivets come in two parts. As in humans and in electric sockets, the parts are referred to as "male" and "female." Rivets are used for all kinds of joinings and are available in small, medium and large, though the large size is used most commonly. For thick jobs, 3/8″ extra-long rivets are available.

*Wax.** Beeswax and black or brown finishing wax are sold in cakes for finishing off edges by sealing and polishing them.

Stains and Dyes. Used for staining or painting on leather. Try to get stains that are marked "indelible."

Coarse Sandpaper and Block. Use your regular household hand-sanding block and a coarse grade of sandpaper.

*Heavy Paper and Transparent Tape.** Use brown wrapping paper and transparent tape for making patterns. For sandal patterns, shirt cardboard or any stiff cardboard will do.

*Chalk and Ball-point Pens. For marking measurements.

Felt-tip Pens. Used for painting or drawing on leather.

Sponges, Q-tips and Paintbrushes. For staining leather.

Rubber Gloves. Used when working with stains.

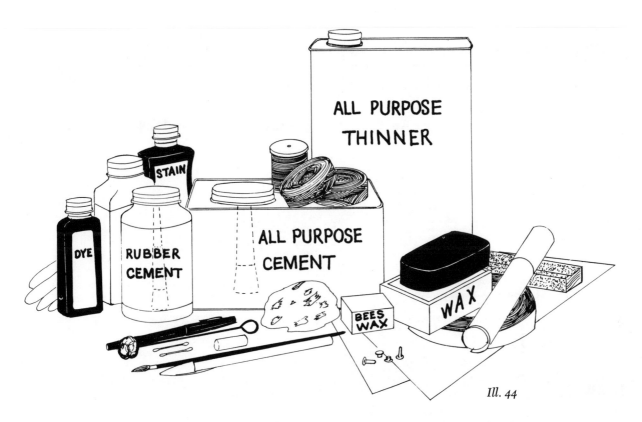

Ill. 44

Hardware and Miscellaneous

You can get these supplies as you need them. Don't invest in a lot of miscellaneous equipment you may never use.

Buckles. These come in hundreds of varieties. Some common types are illustrated on the following page.

A. Tongue—needs no keeper.
B. Peg—no tongue.
C. Tongue.
D. Rings.
E. Sandal buckle.

F. An old metal hinge also makes a nice buckle.

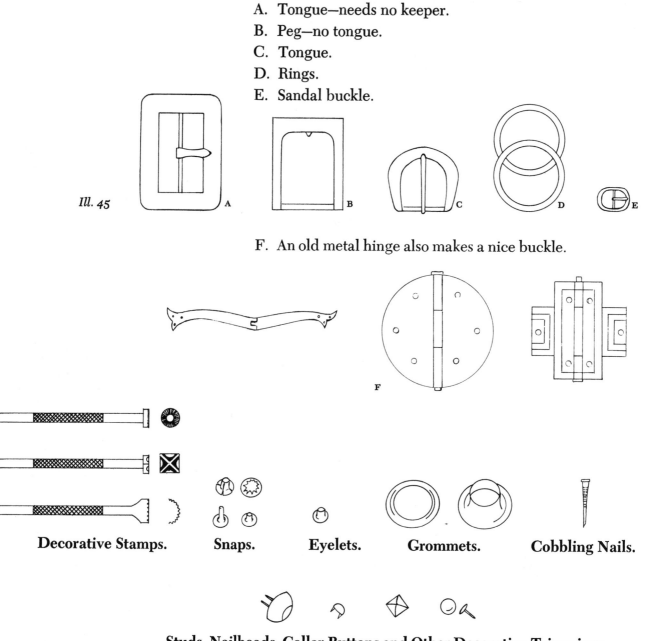

Ill. 45

Decorative Stamps.   Snaps.   Eyelets.   Grommets.   Cobbling Nails.

Studs, Nailheads, Collar Buttons and Other Decorative Trimmings.

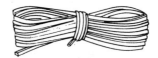

Leather Lacing. Commonly cut in 3/32″ and 1/8″ widths; you can also cut your own.

TECHNIQUES IN LEATHERCRAFT

This section is a review of how the various tools are used to measure, cut, punch, sew, glue and decorate leather. When you come across these techniques in the instructions, you can refer back to this section for anything that isn't familiar to you.

Selecting and Making a Pattern

We have included patterns for making all sorts of things, but they are given here just to help you get started, until you know the possibilities and the limitations of your craft. Don't attempt your own designs until you've worked for a while and can be creative rather than frustrated. It's best to find a design you like or to copy a worn-out handbag or belt you love as a beginning.

Most of our patterns are placed on a grid where each square stands for 1″. The patterns are simple to use:

Take a sheet of heavy paper or cardboard and, with a ruler, divide it into 1″ squares. Now, copy the pattern onto your paper, square for square, as it appears in the book. Cut out your paper pattern. (Of course, in belts or sandals or clothing, adjust to your individual measurement.) Lay the pattern on the leather and tape it in place. If you want, you can outline the pattern on your leather with a ball-point pen, and then remove the pattern, or simply follow the paper pattern when cutting.

Cutting Leather

Most garment-weight (lightweight) leathers can simply be cut with a good pair of scissors. (*Ill. 1*) When working with heavier leathers, you can use a utility knife or bevel knife interchangeably.

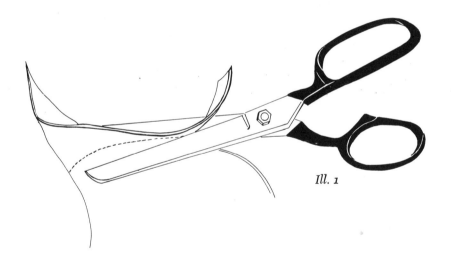

Ill. 1

For straight lines, take a metal square and place it on your leather where you wish the cut to be made. (*Ill. 2*) If you are using a paper pattern, put the metal square on top of the straight lines of your pattern. Grasp the knife firmly and run it along the edge of the square toward you, being very careful with the knife. (*Ill. 3*) If the leather is thick, run the knife over your cutting line again and again until you cut through.

The best way to use the metal square and utility knife is on the cutting board, placed on the floor. Hold your metal square in place,

with your knee on the end closest to you. Place your hand at the top
of the square farthest from you. This holds the square firmly in
place—the square must not move as you cut.

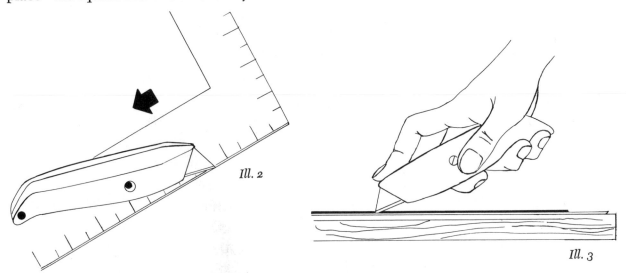

Ill. 2

Ill. 3

If you are cutting a rounded edge, of course you can't use the
straight edge of the metal square. First, make a heavy cardboard
pattern of the shape you want to cut. Place this directly on your
leather. Then grasp the knife firmly and very, very carefully pull the
knife around the edge of your pattern. Make a shallow, light cut to
start with as a guideline. Once this is done, you can apply more
pressure and cut through.

To trim sandal soles, you can use a utility knife as we've described
or, like a shoemaker, you can hold the sandal in one hand and pull a
cobbler's knife, freehand, along the line you want. (*Ill. 4*)

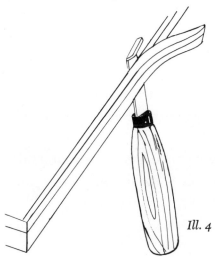

Ill. 4

Belts and Straps

This is the easiest way to cut out belting or strap leather with a knife, using a belt 2″ wide for an example:

1. Cut a straight line against the metal square through the leather with a utility knife. (*Ill. 5, line* A)

2. Move the square 2″ from your starting place, making sure to check with a ruler the distance from the square at the top and bottom to the straight edge of the leather. (*Ill. 5, line* B)

3. Make the second cut 2″ from the first. (*Ill. 6*)

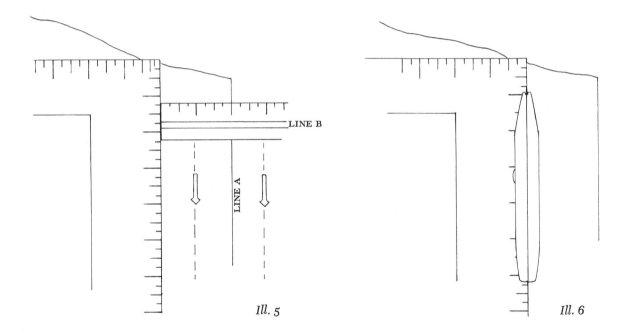

LINE B

LINE A

Ill. 5

Ill. 6

4. Repeat this process until all the necessary straps are cut. Naturally if the piece of leather you are working with is too long for the belt or strap you want, trim off the extra inches, using the metal square and knife. If it is too short, splice two pieces of leather together. (*See page 27.*)

To cut straps with a draw-gauge, first cut a straight line in the leather with a knife. Set the gauge to the desired width. Then hold the gauge in your hand and run it along the straight line of the leather. (*Ill. 7*)

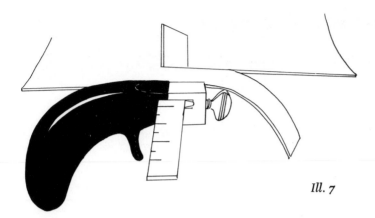

Ill. 7

Splicing and Skiving

This process is used to extend strap lengths. If you want your strap
to be 35″ long and your leather is only 24″, cut two pieces of 24″ long
to the proper width.

Cut one end of each piece to form a 45° angle. Make sure that when
the top side is turned up in both pieces, and the cut ends are placed
together, the angles are *parallel* to each other. Then, allowing for a
1/2″ overlap, measure the two pieces end to end to the 35″ length
you need. (*Ill. 8*)

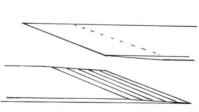

Ill. 8

Ill. 9

You will now have to skive or thin the underside of both angled ends
so that they will fit together neatly and the place where they join will
not show. To do this, use a skife knife with short strokes toward you
in much the same manner as you would use a potato peeler. (*Ill. 9*)
The leather should be shaved 1/2″ in from each end and should taper
from the full thickness of the leather to almost nothing at the angled
end so that the pieces fit together like one. Glue the edges together
according to the instructions on page 40.

To Make Your Own Lacing

If you are using a lightweight leather and want lacing of the same material, you can use the scraps to make lacing. For short pieces, simply cut like straps, but in a narrow width. If you need a rather long lace, take your piece of leather and cut it round and round as if you were peeling an orange, spiral fashion.

Scoring

Leather is scored with a V- or U-shaped cut when you want to make a sharp or definite turn or bend in your work. For example, if you are making a handbag out of heavy cowhide with rounded foldlines, you must score the wrong side first to make the fold easier and to avoid excess bulk.

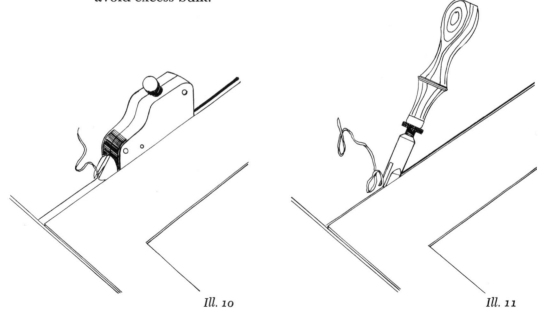

Ill. 10   *Ill. 11*

To score, mark your foldline in the back of the leather with a ball-point pen. The foldlines are indicated on the pattern. Get out your V or U cutting tool. Use your V tool like a small plane, pushing it along the leather as you would push a plane against wood. (*Ill. 10*) The U cutting tool is pushed away from you. (*Ill. 11*) Both tools are adjustable to give you the depth you need, but it's best not to try for a deep cut the first time. Measure the distance from the center of the tool across the blade to the tool's side edge. Place a metal square this distance from the foldline and cut, holding the edge of the tool against the square.

Punching Holes

You make holes in leather to 1) provide a stitching line; 2) apply fasteners; 3) insert straps or; 4) fasten two pieces together.

Decide what kind of holes you need, for stitching or for fastening.

For *stitching*: Before you can stitch you need to mark your leather on the grain side with the line along which the stitching will go. Use

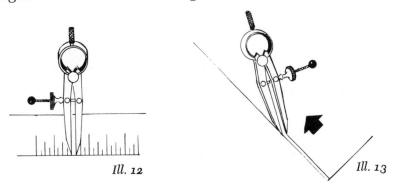

Ill. 12

Ill. 13

your divider to make this straight line. Measure the distance from the edge of leather to where the stitching line will go. Set the divider to this desired width by holding it against a ruler. (*Ill. 12*) Then run it along the leather where the stitching will go. (*Ill. 13*) Make sure your leather is on a flat surface. Of course, you will need to mark in an identical way both pieces of leather which are to be stitched together.

Get out your stump or endgrain block. Place your stitching punch right on the line you've marked on the leather. Hold the leather and the punch on the stump so that the punch will not jump when you hit it. Now take your rawhide mallet and hit the punch firmly so that it goes completely through the leather. (*Ill. 14*)

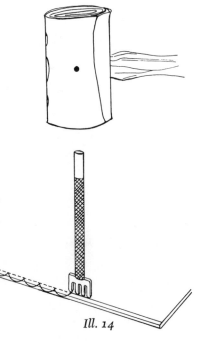

Ill. 14

To move along your marked line, insert the first prong of your punch in the last hole of the group you've just punched. Continue punching for the desired length.

Where your stitching line curves, use a space marker set at the same spacing as the prongs of your punch. Roll it, like a pizza cutter, along the curved lines that you wish to make. (*Ill. 15*) Then take a single-prong punch and, with your mallet, punch each hole separately. (*Ill. 16*)

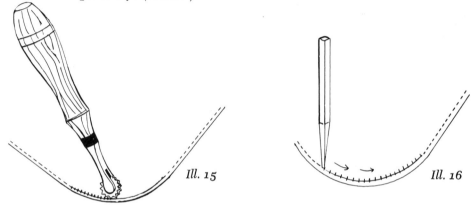

Ill. 15   *Ill. 16*

For *fastening*: Almost all holes for belts and for fasteners are made with a rotary punch. First, decide what size hole you need and mark your leather where the holes are to fall. You can use a ball-point pen or a felt-tip pen to do this. Now, turn your punch so that the cylinder of the correct size is positioned above the copper pad of your punch.

Hold the punch in one hand with the leather between the copper pad and the punch. (*Ill. 17*) Then, grip the handles together firmly. As you do this, the hole will be punched. If a plug of leather is left in the hole, twist the punch before taking it out and the plug will usually come with it. If you want a hole too far from the edge of your leather for your rotary punch to reach, you can use your rotary punch in the same way you would a drive punch, by holding the handles together and placing the tube you want on the leather and opposite the copper pad. Hammer the punch with a rawhide mallet as you would a drive punch, working on a wood stump. (*Ill. 18*) Never punch directly on a tube.

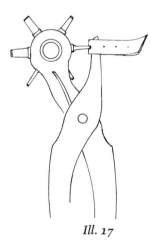

Ill. 17

For larger holes—as for attaching sandal straps—round, oval and oblong drive punches are used.

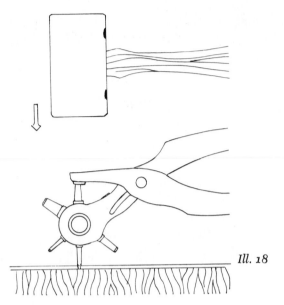

Ill. 18

Decide what shape the hole should be, and then mark your leather where it is to fall. Place it on the stump and grasp the punch very firmly. (*Ill. 19*) You won't punch through sandal leather, for example, on the first stroke, because it is too thick. You will have to punch repeatedly, and it is therefore important that your tool doesn't slip around in your hand. Use a maul rather than a mallet for this work. (*Ill. 20*)

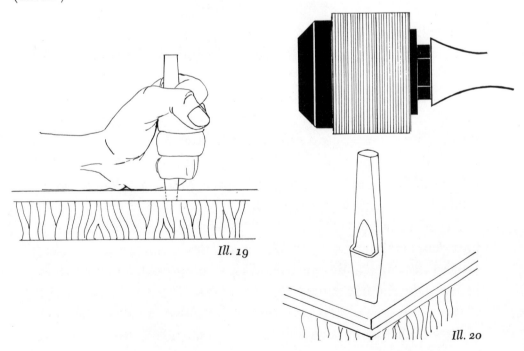

Ill. 19

Ill. 20

Stitching

The simplest stitch, though not the strongest, is the *running stitch.* This is the same running stitch that you use in sewing or basting fabric. (*Ill. 21*)

Ill. 21

To make a running stitch on heavy leather: thread a harness needle with wax thread and stitch in and out through pre-punched holes (*page 29*) just like on fabric. Sometimes, when you are going through several thicknesses of leather, the needle will be hard to pull, even through pre-punched holes. In these cases, take an ordinary pliers and pull your needle through, being careful not to hurt yourself. To end the seam, pull the needle and thread to the inner side of your work and knot or go back over the last stitch.

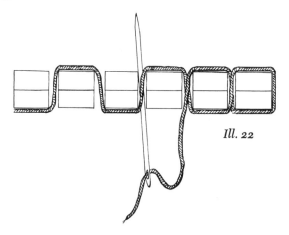

Ill. 22

The *saddle stitch* is a really strong stitch. Many people like the finished look it gives to a piece of work.

To make a saddle stitch quickly: thread a harness needle with wax thread and make a running stitch straight down your seam. Now turn your work around and come back with a running stitch in the spaces between the running stitch already in place. (*Ill. 22*) To make a neater, more even saddle stitch: thread a harness needle at each end of the wax thread. Put one needle through the hole in the leather, but do not pull it. Now push the other needle through the same hole, from the other direction. Pull both needles in opposite directions through the hole. (*Ill. 23*) Pull firmly but not too tightly, keeping an even tension, and your seam won't pucker. (*Ill. 24*) Repeat. To end the seam, stitch back over about four stitches, poke your needle through to the wrong side, and clip the thread.

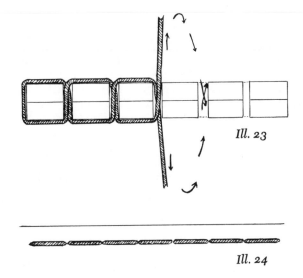

Ill. 23

Ill. 24

The *whipstitch* is used for lacing, finishing, piecing together and decoration. It goes over the edge of your leather.

To whipstitch: It is best to use a slanted prong punch for this stitch, but you *can* use a regular punch. Draw your stitching line and punch your holes as directed (*page 29*). Now slip your lacing through a two-pronged lacing needle and draw it over the top edge of your work into the adjacent hole. Continue working over the edge of your leather, over the top and through the holes to the end of the seam. (*Ill. 25*) To finish your work, draw the lacing to the wrong side of the work and knot.

Ill. 25

Other stitches: When you are comfortable with leathercraft you will find yourself using all sorts of stitches to decorate and fasten your work. For example, on fine leather, you could decorate with large embroidery stitches, or use crochet or macramé to join pieces together.

Using a sewing machine: To make garments, the simplest procedure is to use your sewing machine. For lightweight leather—in most cases, this means soft suede—you can probably use any machine, working in the same manner you would to sew fabrics. Many models include instructions for sewing with leather. Make sure the leather moves through the machine at a fairly long stitch length. (*Ill. 26*)

Use polyester thread in your machine, or heavy-duty cotton thread on heavier leather.

If your machine does not move smoothly along the suede or leather, try putting a sheet of tissue paper *under* the leather where it touches the machine. Sew right through the paper, which is easily ripped off after sewing. If that doesn't work, take each piece that is to be stitched and run it through the machine without thread. Then, line up the two pieces and hand-stitch them together through the holes you've punched with the sewing machine. For information on sewing garments by machine see page 121.

Ill. 26

Setting Eyelets, Rivets, Grommets and Snaps

To make holes for these fastenings, follow the techniques described for punching holes for fastenings (*page 30*), choosing the proper size and shape hole in your rotary or drive punch.

Eyelets are used primarily as lacing fasteners.

To insert eyelets, mark your work where you want the eyelet, and punch the hole with a rotary punch.

Put the eyelet into the hole and through your work on the right side. Place the work, right-side down, on a flat metal surface, either a large one, if you have one, or a spatula or a large coin.

Place the eyelet setter into the eyelet from the wrong side of the leather. Tap the setter with a rawhide mallet. (*Ill. 27*) If you have trouble keeping the eyelet in place, tap a second eyelet inside the first one that has spread. Insert the second eyelet from the wrong side of your work and tap it into place with the setter and rawhide mallet. (*Ill. 28*)

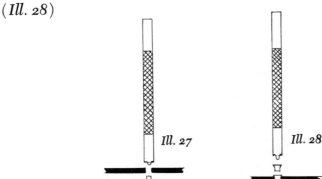

Ill. 27   *Ill. 28*

Rivets are the most commonly used fasteners. They come in two parts, the "female" and the "male."

To insert rivets, mark your work where the rivet is to be placed. Match the female part of your rivet to the hole in your rotary punch by sliding it right into the punch. (*Ill. 29*)

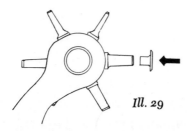

Ill. 29

Punch the two pieces of leather you wish to join with this size hole. In most cases you will be riveting the wrong side of the bottom leather to the wrong side of the top leather. (For example, in riveting a buckle to a belt.) Sometimes, however, you will be riveting wrong side to right side, as in straps for bags and sandals. You will be able to tell from the instructions and illustrations for the individual projects. Insert the male part of the rivet into the hole of the bottom piece of leather, point side up; now place the second piece of leather on top. The male part of the rivet will now stick through the top leather too. (*Ill. 30a*) Place the female part of the rivet over the male. Now turn the work over on a flat metal surface, female side down, and hammer the rivet in place with a metal hammer. (*Ill. 30b*)

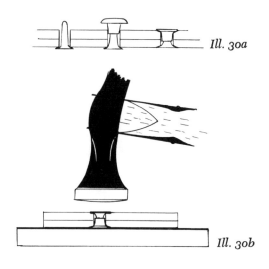

Ill. 30a

Ill. 30b

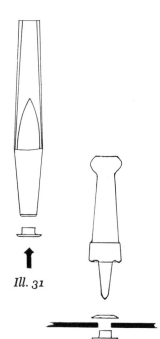

Ill. 31

Ill. 32

Grommets are like sturdy, two-piece eyelets. They are used for lacing or decoration, and can be used through two thicknesses of leather.

To insert grommets, mark the leather where the grommet is to fall and get a drive punch that matches the size of the grommet. As with rivets, the easiest way to measure is to slide the grommet into the drive punch to make sure it fits properly. (*Ill. 31*) Punch your hole in the leather where the grommet is to fall.

Now place the larger half of your grommet into the base of your grommet setter. Place the leather so that the hole is right over the grommet, right side down. Now place the remaining part of the grommet into the hole, cover with the top of the grommet setter, and tap firmly with a rawhide mallet. (*Ill. 32*)

Snaps are used to fasten lightweight leather. You must have a snap setter. The one illustrated on page oo is the cheapest and simplest of these.

A snap has four parts: the top, A and B, and the bottom, C and D. (*Ill. 33*) Mark where the snap is to go on both pieces of your leather. To insert the top of a snap, punch a hole the size of B with a rotary punch. Measure the size of B as you did the rivets.

Line up the two pieces of leather to be fastened together and mark through the hole you have punched to the place where the other part of the snap will fall. Now place B on the largest peg of your setter. Place the leather, wrong side down, so that the hole you have just punched falls on top of B. Now place cap A over B, where it comes through the leather. (*Ill. 33*) Place the concave cylinder of your snap setter over cap A and tap it with a rawhide mallet. (*Ill. 34*) For the other half of your snap, punch your hole in the marked place to fit the size of D. Place D on the smaller peg of your setter. Place the hole in your leather, wrong side down, on top of D. Place C on top of D and on top of the leather. Now take up the smaller cylinder of the setter. Place it on top of D and tap firmly down with a rawhide mallet. (*Ill. 35*)

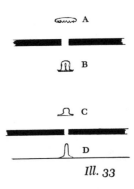

Ill. 33

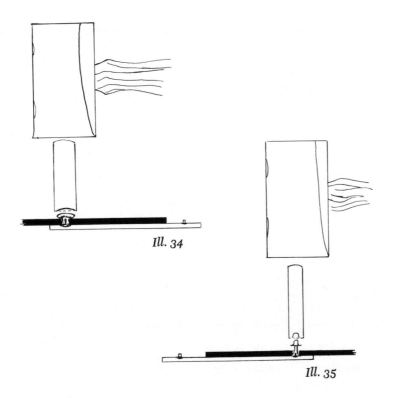

Ill. 34

Ill. 35

Putting on a Buckle

Buckles are used for belts, handbags, sandals, and all sorts of straps. I describe in detail how to place a conventional belt buckle but you can adapt this same method for other work.

The buckle is put in place after the belt is cut and finished (*page 44*).

When working with heavy cowhide, the buckle end of the belt should be skived to eliminate bulk. (*Ill. 36*) Skive the leather 2 1/2″ from the end, tapering it to almost nothing at the very end. If the leather is quite bulky as it fits over the buckle, skive 3 1/2″ from the end. Be careful not to thin this area out too much, since it will carry the stress of the belt. Use a skife knife as described on page 27.

Ill. 36

Mark a dot 2 1/2″ from the end of your belt where the buckle is to go.

Place the belt on an endgrain block or a stump and make a hole over the dot with an oblong punch. This hole will hold the "tongue" part of the buckle. (*Ill. 37*)

Mark a dot on either end of this hole, 1″ from its center.

Mark a dot on either end of these first dots, 1″ away from them. (*Ill. 37*) Now you have four dots lined up around the oblong hole and centered from the sides of the belt.

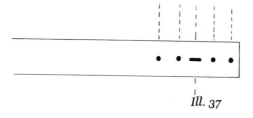

Ill. 37

Punch rivet-sized holes through these four dots with a rotary punch.

Place the tongue of the buckle through the oblong center hole. Pull the leather down on either side of the tongue. (*Ill. 38*)

Fix a rivet (*page 35*) through the hole closest to the tongue. Between this hole and the last one, you will put the belt's keeper, the small band that holds the belt's tail in place. (*Ill. 39*)

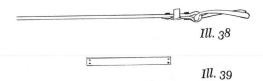

Ill. 38

Ill. 39

To make the keeper, take a finished piece of leather of the width you want and long enough to wrap around two thicknesses of your belt. Fit this piece together end to end, and punch two holes on each end with the small tube of the rotary punch or a single-prong stitching punch. Sew the holes together with a few stitches. Slide the keeper into place onto the belt next to the first rivet. Now fix a rivet through the last hole.

Now that your buckle is in place, you need to make holes on the other end of your belt to fasten it around your waist. You can measure where the holes should go by trying the belt on, marking the place where the tongue fits most comfortably and then evenly spacing a few holes around this first one to allow for expansion or contraction of your waistline. The center hole should be approximately 4″ from the tail end of the belt so that the rivets on the buckle end will be covered. Punch these holes the size of the buckle tongue with a rotary punch. (*Ill. 40*)

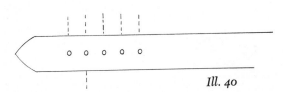

Ill. 40

Now that you know how to fasten a buckle with rivets, you could, if you like, ignore this process and sew your buckle into place.

Bear in mind that certain buckles have different pieces—designed in different ways. I have shown three common varieties here. (*Ill. 41*) Before you begin placing your buckle, figure out how many holes you need to punch. For example, style A in this illustration requires no holes for the keeper, and style B no holes for the tongue.

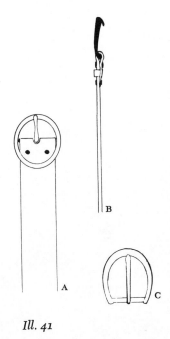

Ill. 41

Cementing

Many projects in leathercraft require gluing, such as sandals, or dress hems. When using rubber cement, it is a good idea to put newspaper under your work so you won't ruin the surface you're working on. Keep the cement container closed when it is not in use so that the glue doesn't evaporate. As we have described earlier, use thinner with your glue when it becomes too thick to run out correctly (*page 20*).

When cementing two small surfaces together, as on belts, use the container's brush applicator. Apply an equal amount of glue to both surfaces—an even amount that is not too globby and not too feathered out. Then cover both surfaces completely. (*Ill. 42*) When the cement is tacky to the touch, place the two surfaces together on some smooth work place. Starting carefully at one end and keeping the sides even, glue together, tapping down the entire length and width with a rawhide mallet. (*Ill. 43*)

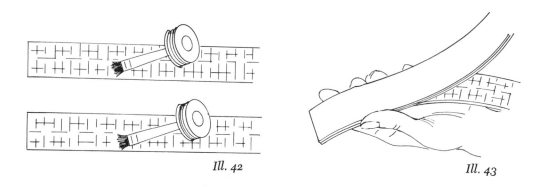

Ill. 42   *Ill. 43*

On heavyweight leather, sole leather, for example, scrape both surfaces with a ruffer before gluing, scraping horizontally and vertically across the surface, making sure the leather doesn't get too stringy. Clip off any strings as necessary. Then, glue the surfaces together, tapping with a mallet as above. If you don't use a ruffer, the glue will not penetrate the leather; instead it will remain on top and the leather will pull apart easily.

To glue large surfaces, like purse linings, pour some glue onto the leather right from the container and spread it around evenly with a piece of stiff cardboard. (*Ill. 44*)

When gluing together large pieces of soft leather, here is a method that will eliminate bulging when you press your surfaces together. Put thin strips of thick cardboard or lath strips about 2″ apart over the glue on your bottom piece. Begin pressing the two surfaces together, starting from one end and working your way to the other end. As you come to the cardboard strips, pull them out, one at a time. (*Ill. 45*)

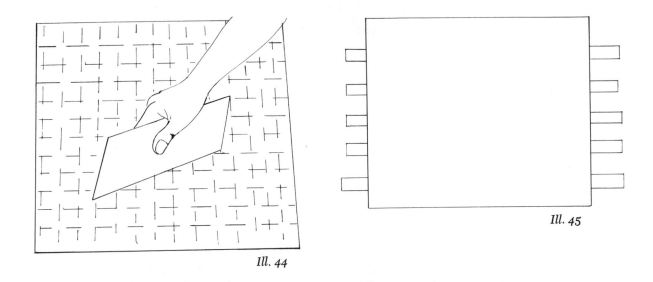

Ill. 44

Ill. 45

Staining

If you wish to stain your leather, do it after cutting but before stitching your pieces together. Wear rubber gloves to protect your hands when you're doing this work.

To stain, make sure your leather is completely clean. If there is any glue on it, the leather won't take the stain evenly.

To apply stain over a large area, pour it into a pie pan. (*Ill. 46*) Put a soft sponge into the pan and then lightly squeeze the sponge so that it is not too full of stain and won't cause an uneven covering on your leather. Place your leather on a flat surface with newspapers

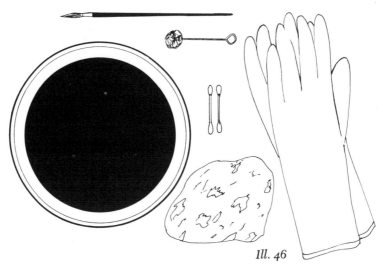

Ill. 46

underneath it. Work the sponge around the leather, either in a circular motion (*Ill. 47*) or by going from side to side. (*Ill. 48*) Both of these techniques give an even, well-covered effect. If you want the stain

Ill. 49

Ill. 47

Ill. 48

to be darker, wait ten or fifteen minutes till the first coat is almost dry and then apply a second coat in the same fashion. When the stain is dry to the touch, rub it with a soft cloth for a nice luster.

For small areas such as holes on a belt, use a Q-tip or paintbrush for staining.

If you apply the stain straight from its bottle with its applicator, press the dauber against the side of the bottle (*Ill. 49*) so you won't get a blot of stain on your leather. If you want a grainy effect, work the dauber from side to side. (*Ill. 50*)

Ill. 50

Appliqués

To make small appliqué pieces to decorate your work, use a bezel shears or an Exacto knife to cut through your leather. First, make a paper pattern of your appliqué design and tape it onto the leather. If you are using scissors or the bezel shears, simply cut around the pattern. (*Ill. 51*) To use the Exacto knife on heavier leather, place your leather on a cutting board, cut down through the pattern and the leather, using a straight edge as your guide in those places where you have straight lines. (*Ill. 52*) The pattern will help prevent soft leather from being pulled along with the knife.

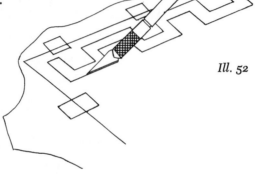

Ill. 52

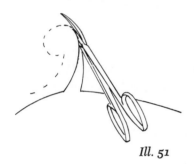

Ill. 51

Drawing or Painting

You can draw on your leather with a felt-tip indelible ink pen in any color you choose. (*Ill. 53*)

Decorative Stamps

Ill. 53

These stamps can be purchased in leathercraft stores and, if they are used imaginatively, they make an interesting decoration. They can be used *only* on natural or vegetable-tanned leather.

Wet your leather thoroughly with water and when it is damp, not wet, place the leather right side up on a flat surface. Make sure your whole piece of leather is moistened before you begin working so that the leather will dry evenly. When it is drying it will lighten in color. Position the stamp where you want the design to fall and strike it firmly with a rawhide mallet. (*Ill. 54*) If your leather doesn't hold the imprint of the stamp, it is probably too wet.

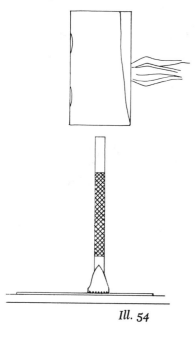

Ill. 54

Edge Finishing

Finishing gives a good, clean look to your work and helps to preserve the leather. It is the difference between a handsome-looking piece of work and a sloppy one. There are commercial edge finishes on the market, but I have found them unsatisfactory. They are often shiny or too plastic looking for leather and many chip or peel with use. Waxing edges may seem laborious, but it seals them and gives a soft luster to the leather.

Edge finishing is done after cementing and sewing. The edges of bags or belts should have been cut with a neat, clean cut. If you find that you are getting a stringy edge—and some leather will do that— trim the edges with a scissors before staining or waxing. If the seams of your bag are not even, sand or trim them to match before finishing.

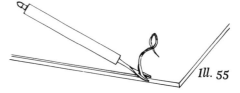

Ill. 55

For a soft edge, use a V-trim or common edger. (*Ill. 55*) You can either stain the edge or leave it its natural color. A cowhide belt would

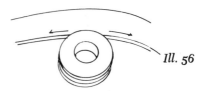

Ill. 56

be finished with a V-trim or common edger in the same way, but should be polished with a hardwood wheel or slick. (*Ill. 56*) To use the slick, rub beeswax over the finished edge and dampen the edge with a sponge. (*Ill. 57*) If the edge has been stained, you can use a matching black or brown wax. After you have waxed the edge, rub vigorously with the slick. For softer leathers a soft cloth may be used. (*Ill. 58*)

Ill. 57   *Ill. 58*

For a decorative line along an unstitched belt or bag edge, you can use an edge creaser. Simply running the edge creaser back and forth in the same groove along your dampened leather will give the leather a finished look. (*Ill. 59*)

When making sandals, you can sand the edge (with a motor, if you've got one), bevel it, stain it, wax and polish it. This technique will be described in more detail in the sandal section on page 107.

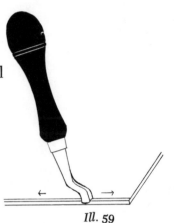

Ill. 59

PROJECTS

Now if you have the materials and tools and know how to use them, you are ready to get on with a project.

Pick something easy to begin with—a belt, perhaps. As you look through the patterns in this book, you'll see that some of them are marked "easy," and these would be good to start with.

Read through the complete instructions for the particular project before you begin and especially before you buy anything—leather or tools. With the pattern, you'll find a list of the materials and tools you'll need, as well as a step-by-step method for each project.

Each pattern is shown in its basic form and laid out on a graph. Following the basic pattern are variations that can be worked without major changes.

To transfer the pattern in the book to your own pattern, follow the instructions on page 23, and you are off.

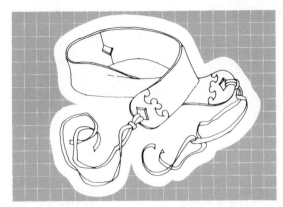

Belts

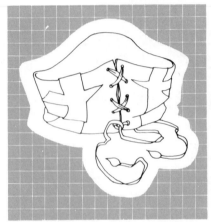

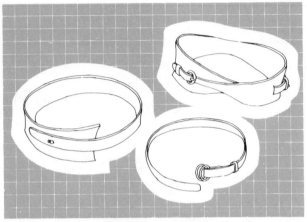

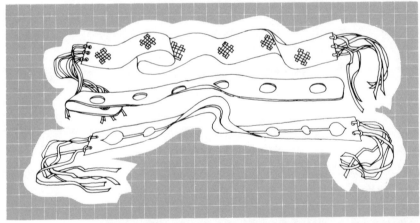

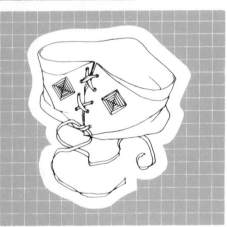

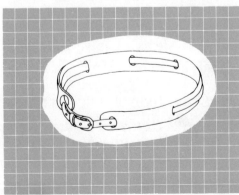

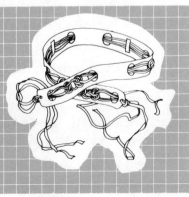

The easiest belts are those made of soft leathers, like suede and cabretta. These can be worked almost like fabric. Cowhide belts are harder to make because you must use a knife to cut the leather and you must finish the edges.

Before you make your belt, measure your waistline with a tape measure and then consult the pattern you are going to be using to see how many inches you must add to your waist size for a particular belt. Bear in mind that a heavy belt will lose a little in its length going around your waist. Don't cut your belt too short. Measure your pattern against a belt that you own which is a perfect fit and use this measurement as a guide.

Of course, if you see a pattern here that you like but wish were wider or narrower, simply make the necessary adjustment as it pleases you and use the appropriate number of fastenings.

Soft Leather Belts

Ill. 3

BASIC TIE BELT / Easy

Suede or soft leather
Leather lacing

This basic belt is one of the easiest belts you can make. It uses no buckle or other hardware, and it is fastened simply by the addition of ties, like a scarf or some macramé, or leather thongs.

1. Make a paper pattern (page 23) from the dimensions on the graph and to your waist specifications. (*Ill. 1*)

2. Take a piece of leather, double the width you want your finished belt to be. Lay the leather out on a flat surface. Cut out your paper pattern and tape it to the right side of your leather. Use several small

pieces of tape, rather than attempting to run one length of tape evenly down the side of the pattern.

3. With your scissors, cut out the belt, snipping right through the tape.

4. Turn your belt to the wrong side. With a ball-point pen, draw a line down the center, going the full length of the belt. Then draw two lines equidistant from this center line, and from the two edges, the length of the belt.

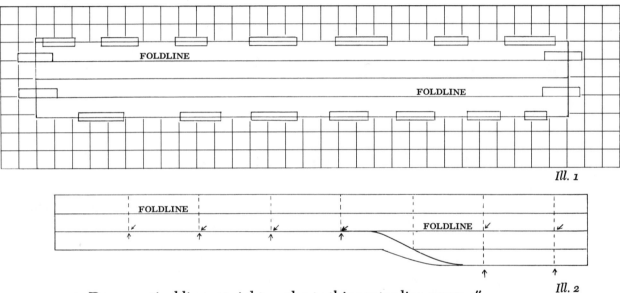

FOLDLINE

FOLDLINE

Ill. 1

FOLDLINE

FOLDLINE

Ill. 2

5. Draw vertical lines at right angles to this center line every 4", on the wrong side, of course. These vertical lines will serve as the guide to keep the edge from stretching when you glue. (*Ill. 2*)

6. Place the belt horizontally in front of you with the right side down. Cover the entire *wrong* side, including the edges, with rubber cement. Let the belt stand until the glue is tacky to the touch.

7. Starting at the extreme left end of the belt, fold the bottom edge to the center line, pressing down with your fingers as you move down the length of the belt. Match the edge of the leather to the center line at each vertical line. (*See arrows in Ill. 2*) When this fold is entirely in place, fold the top edge down to the center line and glue in the same manner.

8. Place the belt on a smooth surface and tap the entire wrong side with a rawhide mallet to flatten and seal. Trim the ends for a perfect match.

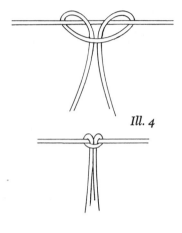

9. Now punch two holes at each end of your belt with the largest tube of your rotary punch (*page 30*).

10. Take a piece of leather lacing long enough so that when it is inserted through the holes you can easily tie your belt. You can use leather lacing of the same color or a contrasting color, as you like. Knot the pieces of lacing through the holes that you have punched and fasten them with a lark's head knot. (*Ill. 4*)

Ill. 4

TIE BELT WITH CUTOUTS / Easy

Suede or soft leather
Leather lacing

1. Make the belt exactly as you made the tie belt, working through step 8.

2. Round the ends of your belt slightly with scissors.

Ill. 5

3. Draw an *even* number of holes on the wrong side of the belt of any size that pleases you. Center the holes on the belt and make sure they are evenly spaced. Cut out these holes with your bezel shears.

4. Punch one hole, centered, at either end of your belt with the largest tube of your rotary punch (*page 30*).

5. Knot the pieces of leather lacing as in the basic tie belt.

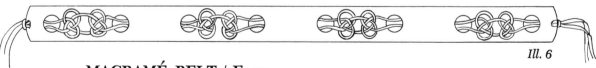

Ill. 6

MACRAMÉ BELT / Easy

Suede or soft leather
Macramé cord

1. Make the belt exactly as you did for the tie belt with cutouts, except for step 5.

2. Use macramé cord to lace through the holes all around the belt. You will find macramé knots in any good book on the subject. I have illustrated here the Josephine knot.

3. To keep the cord from slipping through the holes, put a dot of cement on the back of your belt under the cord at the sides of each hole.

4. Knot the ties with macramé cord instead of leather lacing.

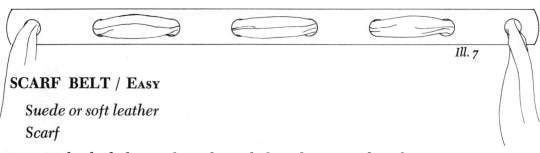

Ill. 7

SCARF BELT / Easy

Suede or soft leather
Scarf

1. Make the belt exactly as the tie belt with cutouts, but eliminate steps 4 and 5.

2. Instead, take a very long scarf of a color that goes well with your leather and thread it neatly through the holes.

3. Tie your belt at the center with the ends of the scarf.

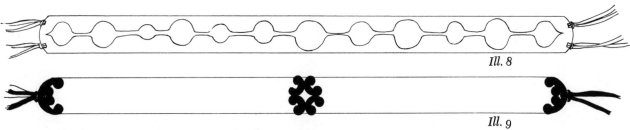

Ill. 8

Ill. 9

TIE BELT WITH APPLIQUÉ / Easy

Suede or soft leather
Contrasting color leather for appliqués
Leather lacing

These belts are merely decorated versions of the basic tie belt.

1. Make the belt exactly as you made the basic tie belt, working through step 8, but rounding both ends.

2. Work out an appliqué pattern you like. Cut out a paper pattern to your design. Tape this paper pattern onto your appliqué leather and cut out the appliqués with the bezel shears.

3. Position the appliqués on the right side of your belt where you want them to fall. Mark their shapes onto the belt with an awl, making a light, neat guideline. Remove the appliqués.

4. Apply rubber cement to the back of each appliqué and *very carefully* inside the guideline you've marked on your belt. When the cement is tacky, carefully place the appliqué in position on the belt. Tap gently with a rawhide mallet to fix the appliqués in place.

(It is really better, but a lot more trouble, to stitch the appliqués onto your belt with a sewing machine, using a zigzag stitch (*Ill. 10*) or a straight stitch. (*Ill. 11*) However, if you are going to stitch the appliqués on, the work must be done *before* the belt is doubled and cemented in back.)

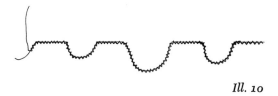

Ill. 10

5. Using the largest tube of your rotary punch, make two holes (*page 30*) at each end of the belt in illustration 8. Cut lacing (*page 28*) of the same leather as your appliqués and knot the lacing through the holes you've punched with a lark's head knot (*page 52*).

Ill. 11

For the belt in illustration 9, the holes—only one at each end—are cut with a scissors right through the appliqué at the ends of the belt. Tie with a lark's head knot as in the basic tie belt.

NEEDLEPOINT BELT / Intermediate

Suede or soft leather
Leather lacing

This belt is the basic tie belt decorated with needlepoint that is done with a glover's needle.

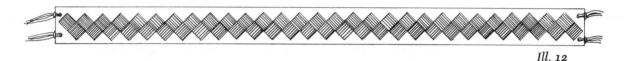

Ill. 12

1. Make the belt exactly as you would the basic tie belt, working through step 5.
2. Before cementing the edges of your belt as in the basic instructions, draw the design shown in illustration 13 (or any other simple needlepoint design) on the right side of the belt with an awl. Make sure the pattern is placed in the middle of the belt after the edges are turned under.

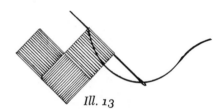

Ill. 13

3. Work the needlepoint as you would on fabric, using a glover's needle.
4. Complete the belt as in the instructions for the basic tie belt, beginning with step 6.

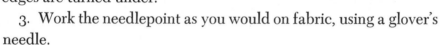

Ill. 14

LONGEVITY KNOT BELT / Advanced

Suede or soft leather
Strips of suede, yarn or rope
Leather lacing

The design of this belt, called a Longevity Knot, is a bit complex, but it is very, very nice looking. The Longevity Knot can be made with strips of suede, yarn or rope woven through the belt.

1. Make the belt as you made the basic tie belt, working through step 5.

2. Get some graph paper with 1/8″ squares. Mark the holes on the paper as in illustration 15 and punch the holes out of the paper.

3. Lay the graph paper on your leather where you want the design to fall.

4. Before cementing the edges of your belt, mark all the dots in your paper pattern on the right side of the leather with a ball-point pen, moving the paper design and marking down the length of the belt. Be careful to center the pattern and to allow for turning the edges.

5. Set the rotary punch to the size hole that will fit your yarn or lacing. Punch out (*page 30*) the penned dots.

6. Weave your strips of suede, yarn or rope through the holes, using a glover's needle. Work your thread over and under, following the sequence indicated in illustration 16. Note that in position 1 in the illustration, your needle is coming up from the underside to the top of the belt. This is important if the design is to work out properly. Now complete the pattern by filling in the two corners and connecting 2 and 3, 4 and 5, 8 and 9, and 10 and 11.

7. When all your knots have been worked, finish as in the basic tie belt.

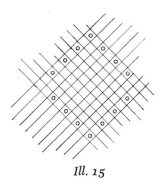

Ill. 15

Ill. 16

BASIC CINCH BELT / Easy

Suede or soft leather
Leather lacing

The basic belt is a soft midriff cinch, laced up the front.

1. Choose the style of cinch belt you like and make a paper pattern from the dimensions on the graph in the following manner:

    A. Determine your waist specifications, then fold your paper to half of that dimension.

    B. Draw half your belt onto the paper, placing the center back of the belt at the fold. (*Ill. 17*)

    C. When this is cut out, each side of your belt will be identical.

2. Unfold the paper pattern, tape it to your leather, and cut it out with scissors.

3. Punch the holes (*page 30*) for your style belt with the largest tube of your rotary punch at each end of the belt as in the illustration. If you want to put in eyelets, do so, matching the size of the eyelet to the rotary punch (*page 35*). It is best, before punching out the holes, to cement an extra strip of your leather to the wrong side of the front edges to provide extra strength and rigidity at this stress point. This is especially important if you choose not to use eyelets.

4. Thread lacing through these holes and knot with a lark's head knot (*page 52*) or by looping the lacing back and forth in a pattern that pleases you.

Ill. 17

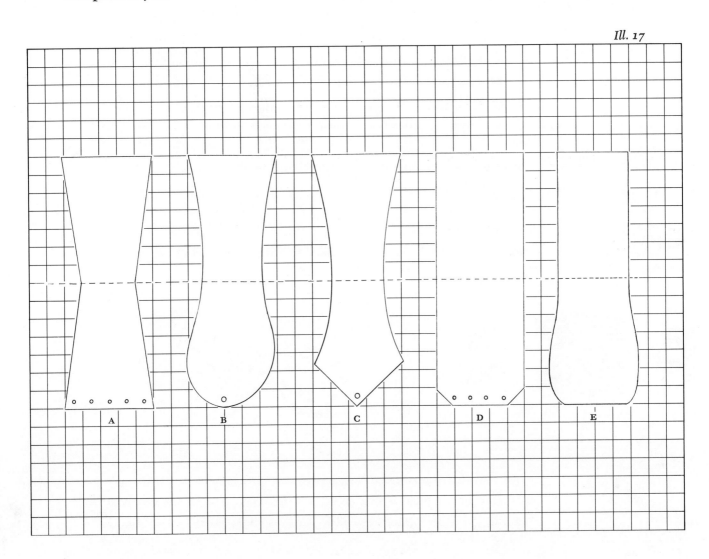

CINCH BELT WITH DIAMOND APPLIQUE / INTERMEDIATE

Suede or soft leather
Contrasting suede for appliqué
Leather lacing
Heavy yarn

This belt is made with two different colored pieces of suede. The belt itself is done in one color and the elongated diamonds are appliquéd on top in another color.

1. Make the belt exactly as you made the basic cinch belt, using illustration 17, style A, and working through step 3.

2. On a piece of paper, cut an appliqué pattern of one elongated diamond and two triangles as shown in illustration 18A. Cut out this paper pattern and tape it to your appliqué leather. Cut out the appliqués with scissors and position them on the right side of your belt, where you want them to fall. Mark their shape onto the belt with an awl, making a neat, light guideline. Remove appliqués.

3. In the center of each appliqué, mark four holes which will form squares on the diagonal, as shown. Punch out these holes (*page 30*) with the smallest hole on your rotary punch. String yarn through these holes, forming a cross. (*Ill. 19*)

4. At this point, apply rubber cement to the back of your appliqués and, very carefully, inside the guidelines marked on your belt. When the cement is tacky, carefully place the appliqués into position on the belt. Tap them gently with a rawhide mallet.

Ill. 18

5. Now fill out your crosses with yarn as shown in illustration, winding the yarn clockwise over the top of one arm of the cross, going behind, over the top and onto the next, as shown. (*Ill. 20*) When the

cross has been filled out, tuck the loose end under it and cement
it down.

6. Now thread lacing through the tie holes and knot with a lark's
head knot (*page 52*) or by looping the lacing back and forth in a
pattern that pleases you.

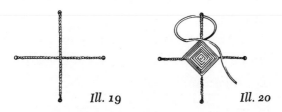

Ill. 19   Ill. 20

OTHER CINCH BELT WITH APPLIQUÉS / INTERMEDIATE

Suede and soft leather
Contrasting suede for appliqué
Leather lacing

1. Make the belt exactly as you made the basic cinch belt, using
the appropriate style from illustration 17 and working through step 3.

2. Work out appliqué patterns for these belts, adjusting your designs
to scale from our graph onto your pattern paper. (*Ill. 21*) You can,
of course, design your own appliqué. Cut out your paper pattern and
tape to the appliqué leather. Cut out the appliqués with scissors.

3. Position the appliqués where you want them to fall on the right
side of your belt. Mark their shape onto the belt with an awl, making
a light, neat guideline. Remove appliqués.

4. Apply rubber cement to the back of the appliqués and, very
carefully, inside the guidelines you have marked. When the cement
is tacky, carefully place the appliqués in position on the belt and tap
them gently with a rawhide mallet.

5. Thread lacing through the holes.

6. I have fastened the belt shown in illustration 18, style C, with an
old hinge, working it into the design. However, you can finish with a
lark's head knot (*page 52*) or with any other kind of decorative
fastening.

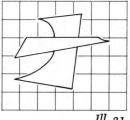

Ill. 21

CINCH BELT WITH PIPING / Advanced

Suede or soft leather
Leather lacing
Rayon or synthetic lining fabric
Cording or piping

1. This belt is meant to fit around your waist exactly, just meeting at the front. Make a paper pattern for the basic cinch belt, using illustration 17, style E. Use your waistline measurement for the belt's length. The belt can be as wide or as narrow as you like, but add a 1/2″ seam allowance all around the belt.

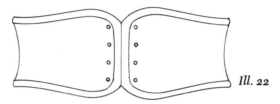

Ill. 22

2. Tape the paper pattern to your leather and cut it out with scissors. Cut a piece of lining fabric to this shape. Cut a piece of cording the length of the outline of the whole belt, plus 2″. Cut a strip the same length and 1 1/2″ wide, of the leather used for the belt or leather of a contrasting color.

3. Cover the cording with the leather strip by gluing the strip over the cording and then stitching it tightly along the cording to within 1 1/2″ of each end as illustrated. (*Ill. 23*) Trim the seam allowance to 1/2″.

Ill. 23

4. Starting at the back of the belt, on the lower edge, place the covered cording along the edge of the belt, with the raw edges of both pieces together.

5. On the seam allowance only, tack the belt and cording together with cement, working all around the belt. When you get back to the place you started, cut the end of the cording, *not* its leather casing, to just meet the other end. Glue in place with a spot of cement. Now cut the leather casing at an angle so it fits neatly together with a slight overlap, as in illustration 24.

Ill. 24

6. Snip into the cord and the belt's seam allowance on all the curves around the belt, as shown by V's in illustration 25. This will permit the

cording to lie flat and will take away the bulk in the seam allowance when it is turned inside out.

7. Make stitching holes with your prong punch and stitch the cording to the belt, sewing on top of the original stitching line next to the cording.

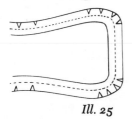

Ill. 25

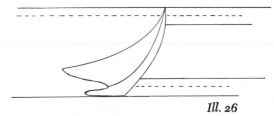

Ill. 26

8. Place the lining on the belt, right side of belt to right side of lining. Tack the lining in place with rubber cement on the seam allowance. Stitch the lining to the belt, leaving 4″ open at the center bottom of the belt. (*Ill. 26*)

9. Turn the belt right side out through the open 4″ and stitch this part in place by hand.

10. With a rotary punch, punch holes (*page 30*) for lacing, as shown in illustration 22. Insert eyelets (*page 35*) in the punched holes.

11. Thread lacing through the tie holes.

CINCH BELT WITH CORDING / ADVANCED

Suede or soft leather
Cording or piping
Lacing (optional)

This belt uses cording in a different way.

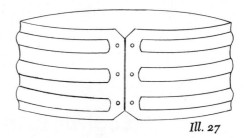

Ill. 27

1. This belt should just fit your waist and fasten at the front. Make a paper pattern as for the basic cinch belt, using illustration 17, style D. Use your waistline measurements for the belt's length, making it as wide as you like.

2. Tape the paper pattern to your leather and cut it out with scissors. Cut another pattern and piece of leather, 1 1/2″ wider and 1/2″ longer than the first piece. Cut three pieces of cording, 2″ shorter than the pattern's length.

3. Place the cording evenly spaced on the reverse side of the smaller piece of leather, beginning 1″ from the end and running the length of the piece but stopping 1″ from the opposite end. (*Ill. 28*) Glue the cording in place.

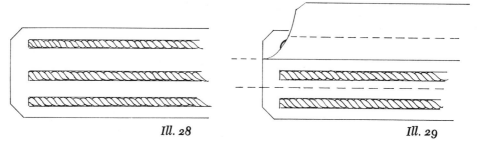

Ill. 28   *Ill. 29*

4. Now glue the back of the larger piece of leather to the back of the smaller piece, working down from the top, molding the leather around one strip of cording at a time. Make sure the leather is fitted snugly over the cording, working your fingers around each side of the cording for a nice raised effect. (*Ill. 29*)

5. Stitch around the cording as close as possible to outline it on the show side of the belt, if you like. (*Ill. 30*)

6. If necessary trim the edges of leather to match.

7. With a rotary punch, punch holes (*page 30*) for lacing. Insert lacing with lark's head knots (*page 52*) or with eyelets.

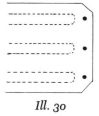

Ill. 30

Cowhide Belts

Cowhide belts are made differently from those of suede or soft leathers simply because cowhide is a much heavier leather, requiring different tools and techniques. As you will see, you may choose from a variety of types of cowhide for many of these patterns. Some of the patterns require buckles, which may be found in antique shops, in junk stores, at garage sales, in leathercraft shops, and in notions stores, as well as in your own dresser drawers.

LOOP BELT / Easy

Oil- or chrome-tanned cowhide

This belt is an easy one to try for your first attempt at working with cowhide. As you will see, it uses no hardware at all.

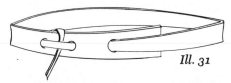

Ill. 31

1. Make up a paper pattern (*page 23*) from the dimensions on the graph. (*Ill. 32*) This belt should be 2″ wide at one end and tapered to 1/4″ at the other. Its length should be your waist measurement *plus* 20″.

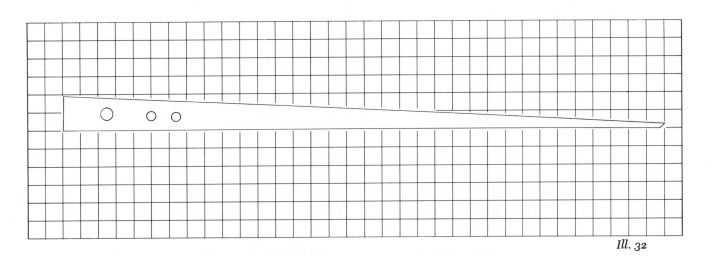

Ill. 32

2. Lay out your leather, cut out the paper pattern and tape it to the right side of the leather. Cut out the belt with a utility knife, placing the metal square at the top of your pattern as a cutting guide (*page 24*).

3. Punch three holes (*page 30*) with a round drive punch. The first one, at the wide end, should be centered and spaced 2 1/2″ from the end of the belt. It should be 5/8″ big. Hole #2 should be 2 1/2″ from the first and be of the 1/2″ size. Hole #3 should be 1 1/2″ from hole #2 and 1/2″ in size.

4. Finish the edge of the belt (*page 44*) and wax.

5. To fasten the belt, thread the smallest end of the belt through the 3 holes as shown. (*Ill. 31*)

BELT WITH COLLAR BUTTON / Easy

Oil- or chrome-tanned cowhide

1. Make up the paper pattern (*page 23*) from the dimensions on the graph. (*Ill. 34*) This belt should be 2 1/2″ wide at one end and tapered to 5/8″ at the other. The length should be your waist measurement *plus 9 1/2″*.

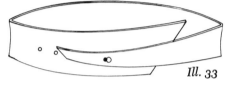

Ill. 33   Ill. 35

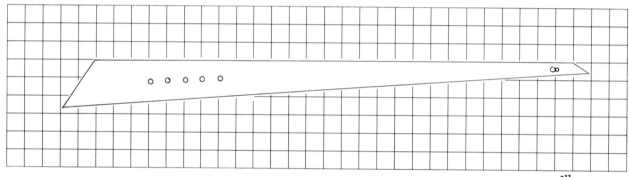

Ill. 34

2. Lay out the leather, cut out the paper pattern and tape it to the right side of the leather. Cut out the belt as in the loop cowhide belt.

3. Punch five holes at one end of the belt and one hole at the other. These holes should be made with the rotary punch (*page 30*) to a size a bit smaller than the ball of your collar button. (*Ill. 35*) In order to do this, fit the ball end of your collar button to the tube that matches its size. Punch the five holes with this tube on the fat end of the belt, centered and equally spaced. Punch one hole of the same size 2 1/2″ from the other end of the belt, again centering it. Make a smaller hole, the size of the collar button stem, to join this single hole, as shown in the graph. This is where the collar buttton will rest when the belt is secured. (*Ill. 33*)

4. Put the collar button in place. Because the collar button has a flange at the bottom it remains in place. No gluing or stitching is required.

5. Finish the edge of the belt (*page 44*) and wax.

BASIC BUCKLE BELT / Easy

Natural cowhide,
oil- or chrome-tanned cowhide,
or heavy calf

1. Make up a paper pattern (*page 23*) to your waist specifications and from the dimensions on the graph. (*Ill. 36*) Tape the pattern to your leather. Cut out the belt with the utility knife, using a metal square as your guide.

2. Stain the belt now, if you like.

3. Finish the edges (*page 44*) and wax.

4. The buckle for this belt needs no keeper. (*Ill. 37*) Follow instructions in the section on buckles (*page 38*) for the exact placement and attachment of your buckle, including the holes for the belt's tongue.

Ill. 37

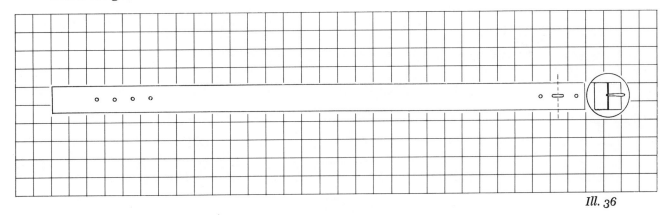

Ill. 36

STITCHED BELT WITH BUCKLE / Intermediate

Natural cowhide,
oil- or chrome-tanned cowhide,
or heavy calf

The only difference between this belt and the previous buckle belt is that this one has double rivets at the buckle, is stitched all around, and has a V-shaped end.

1. Make up a paper pattern (*page 23*) to your waist specifications and from the dimensions on the graph. (*Ill. 38*) Cut a cardboard pattern for this V-shaped end to make it easier to work with. Tape the pattern to your leather. Using a metal square for a guide, cut out the belt with the utility knife.

2. If you use the kind of buckle in illustration 39, you will need a keeper. (*Ill. 40*) Cut one out of your leather, making sure it goes around two thicknesses of your belt.

3. Stain the belt if you like (*page 41*).

4. With the stitching punch, pre-punch holes (*page 29*) completely around the belt. Stitch with waxed thread, using either the running stitch or saddle stitch.

5. Finish the edges (*page 44*) and wax.

6. Follow instructions in the section on buckles for placement and attachment of your buckle and keeper (*page 38*), including the holes for the belt's tongue.

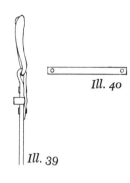

Ill. 40

Ill. 39

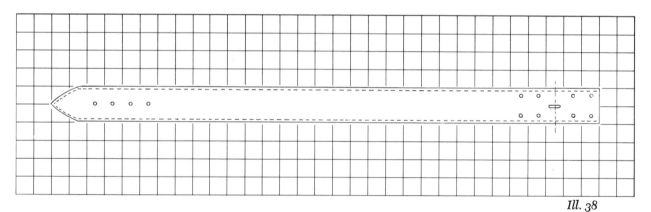

Ill. 38

RING BELT / Easy

Natural cowhide,
oil- or chrome-tanned cowhide,
or heavy calf

This is the simplest belt of the group to make, but it is the most complicated to figure out once you're wearing it. Purchase a belt ring of appropriate size for the width of belt you want.

1. Make up a pattern (*page 23*) to your waist specifications and from the dimensions on the graph. (*Ill. 41*) Notice that there are no holes and that one end of the belt is rounded.

2. Skive the ring end of the belt (*page 27*).

3. With your stitching punch, make holes as indicated on the pattern. Stitch the rings in place (*Ill. 42*), according to stitching instructions (*page 32*).

4. Stain if you wish.

5. Finish the edges (*page 44*) and wax.

Ill. 42

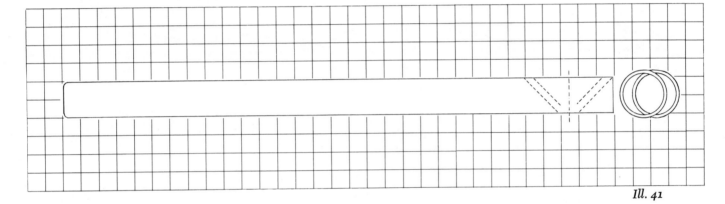

Ill. 41

LACED BELT / ADVANCED

Natural cowhide,
   oil- or chrome-tanned cowhide, or heavy calf
Leather lacing

1. Make your pattern (*page 23*) to your waist specifications and from the dimensions on the graph. (*Ill. 43*) Tape the pattern on the leather and cut it out with the utility knife and metal square.

2. Skive the end of the belt and punch holes for the buckle rivets, according to instructions on page 38.

3. With your drive punch, punch holes (*page 30*) the size of your grommets for the lacing, as in illustration 43. Put small grommets in these holes (*page 36*).

4. Stain and finish the edges of your belt.

5. Rivet (*page 35*) and glue the ring in place.

6. Knot two strips of lacing together at one end. Starting on the underside of your belt, pull the lacing through the first hole to the knot. Now glue the knot in back. Then, working with each lace separately, lace to the last hole and pull both ends to the underside.

7. Try the belt on to make sure the lacing is not pulled too tightly. Knot the lacing and glue the knot in place on the wrong side of the belt.

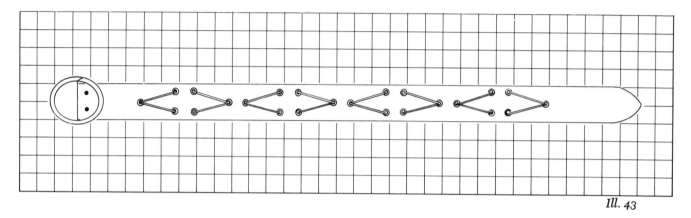

Ill. 43

RECTANGLE BELT / ADVANCED

Lightweight cowhide
Leather lacing

1. Make a paper pattern for the size of the rectangles. (*Ill. 44*) Determine how many rectangles you will need to fit around your waist comfortably. Cut these rectangles out of leather with the utility knife and metal square. (This belt looks particularly nice when the rectangles are stained in contrasting colors.)

2. With your rotary punch, punch two holes the size of your grommets (*page 30*) at both ends of each rectangle. For the rectangle which is to hold the buckle, punch only two holes and for the rectangle which is to fasten to the buckle, punch eight holes as shown in the illustration.

3. Set your grommets in place (*page 36*).

4. Finish the edges (*page 44*).

5. Attach a buckle according to instructions on page oo.

6. String the rectangles together with a long strip of cowhide, working in and out as if you were sewing. Start at the buckle end and

go all the way to the end at the top of the rectangles. Then work back along the bottom line. Knot each end on the underside.

7. Attach buckle (*page 38*).

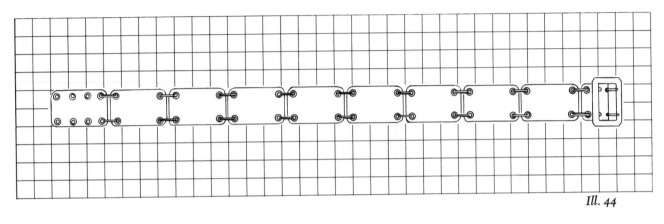

Ill. 44

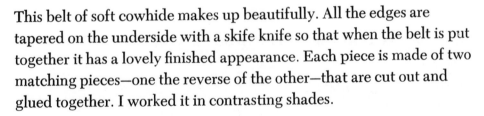

ITALIAN-STYLE BELT / ADVANCED

Oil- or chrome-tanned cowhide

This belt of soft cowhide makes up beautifully. All the edges are tapered on the underside with a skife knife so that when the belt is put together it has a lovely finished appearance. Each piece is made of two matching pieces—one the reverse of the other—that are cut out and glued together. I worked it in contrasting shades.

1. Make up paper patterns (*page 23*) from the dimensions on the graph, for pieces No. 1 and No. 2. (*Ill. 46*) Tape the patterns to the leather and cut out four pieces, two of each pattern, with your utility knife and metal square.

Ill. 46

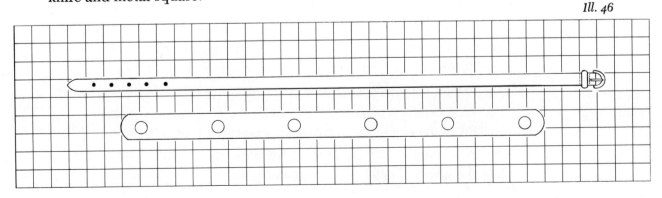

2. Turn all the pieces of the belt wrong side up and skive (*page 27*) all the edges. (*Ill. 47*) In cross section, the matching pieces should fit together as in illustration 48. Skive the end for the buckle, as well as the opposite end. Glue the two parts of each section together and tap with a rawhide mallet. Illustration 49 shows how the pieces will look when they have been hammered together.

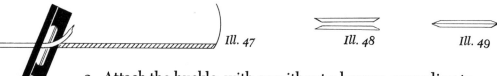

Ill. 47 Ill. 48 Ill. 49

3. Attach the buckle, with or without a keeper, according to instructions on page 38. Make the holes for the belt's tongue.

4. On piece No. 2, punch holes with a drive punch, according to scale on the graph.

5. Put the two pieces together by threading the long piece through the holes in the short piece. (*Ill. 45*)

CRISS-CROSS ITALIAN-STYLE BELT / Advanced

Ostrich
Medium-weight cowhide
Calf lining

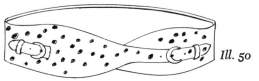

Ill. 50

1. Make up a pattern (*page 23*) for three pieces (*Ill. 51*) according to the graph. Adjust the pattern to your waist specifications.

2. From your cowhide, cut one No. 1 piece for the body of the belt. Cut another No. 1 piece from the calf lining. Cut a third No. 1 piece, adding a 3/8″ seam allowance all the way around, from your ostrich. Use the utility knife to cut the cowhide, but be careful around the corners. Scissors can be used to cut the ostrich and calf lining.

3. From the cowhide, cut two No. 2 pieces, which will hold the buckle.

4. From the cowhide, cut two No. 3 pieces, which will be the keepers. From the ostrich, cut two No. 2 pieces and two No. 3 pieces, all of them with a 3/8″ seam allowance.

5. Skive (*page 27*) your cowhide No. 1 piece 1/8″ from the top edge, all around the edge of the piece. (*Ill. 52*)

6. Glue your No. 1 ostrich piece over the No. 1 cowhide piece with the wrong side of the ostrich to the right side of the cowhide, wrapping the seam allowance on the ostrich piece neatly around all the cowhide edges. This will reinforce the ostrich. After you've pulled the seam allowance around the cowhide, glue it in the back. If you wet the ostrich before you glue it, it will shrink as it dries and tighten around the cowhide for a good fit.

Ill. 52

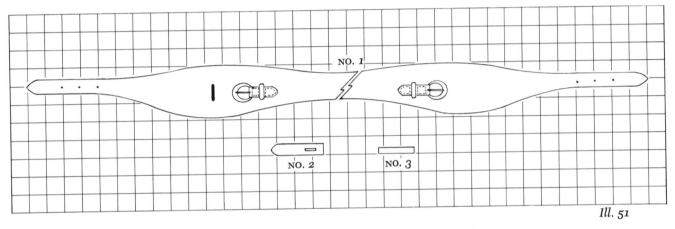

Ill. 51

7. Glue the calf lining to the back of the belt so that it covers the ostrich's seam allowance. (*Ill. 53*) Illustration 54 shows the three pieces of leather in cross section.

8. In the same place as marked on the graph, with an oblong punch, punch (*page 30*) the slit for one end of the belt to go through. Punch holes for the buckle's tongue on both ends of piece No. 1.

Ill. 53

Ill. 54

9. Cover cowhide pieces Nos. 2 and 3, the buckle holder and keeper, with the corresponding ostrich pieces, pulling the seam allowance to the back and gluing as you did with piece No. 1. Punch a hole with your oblong punch in the No. 2 pieces.

Ill. 55

10. Insert the buckles into both No. 2 pieces and stitch them with the keeper in place (*page 38*) on the top of the belt, as shown in illustration 55.

Bags

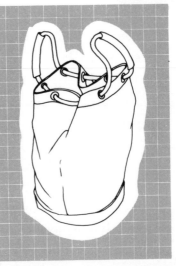

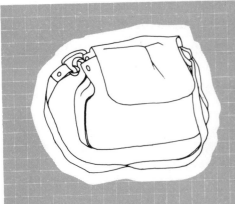

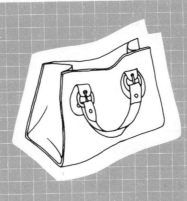

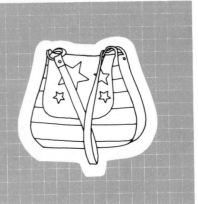

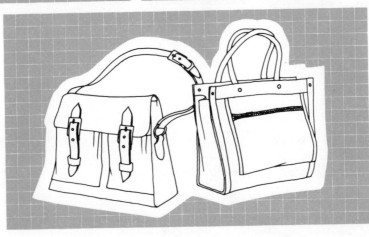

To buy a really good-looking and useful handbag is an expensive proposition, as everybody knows. Once you get the basic technique of making your own, you're going to find making bags both very economical and fairly simple.

Hand and shoulder bags come in a variety of shapes and sizes, for men as well as women. All the bags in this chapter are designed with simplicity in mind and with the idea of getting you started making and designing your own. Once you have made a couple of bags, you'll see how easy they are and you can then go on to create your own patterns.

Before you start any particular design, read through all the directions for that bag first. Make your own paper pattern from the graph according to the instructions on page 23. Remember the rule that we've been using throughout the book: each square in our pattern equals one inch. Your pattern should be cut on heavy brown paper, then taped to your leather and cut out with scissors or a knife, depending on the thickness of the leather. When you are machine-stitching pieces of a bag together, tape the edges together first or fasten them with paper clips before you begin to stitch.

You can change the dimensions of any bag in this book to fit your own needs. Simply remember to scale the pieces so that the seams match.

Ill. 1

NOTE CASE / Easy

Cowhide, kip, heavy suede or latigo

Both this bag and the bag which follows are made from the same basic pattern, though they use the pattern pieces somewhat differently. The bodies are put together in much the same manner. The bags are fairly simple and have been designed with the idea of getting you started on these projects. The fronts of these bags can either be decorated or left plain.

1. Make your paper pattern (*page 23*) according to illustration 2, and tape it to the leather.

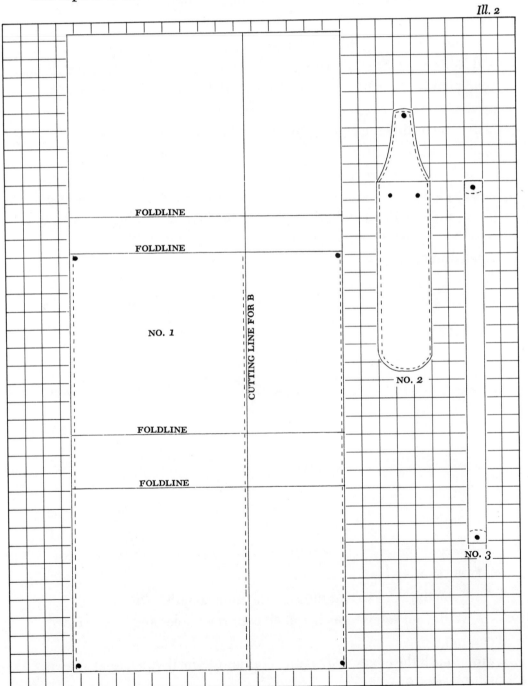

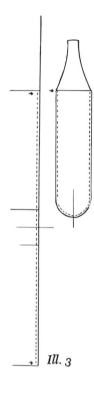

Ill. 3

2. Cut out one full No. 1 piece, using a utility knife and metal square, and mark the foldlines on the wrong side of the leather.

3. Cut two No. 2 pieces but cut *only* up to the straight line indicated on the illustration.

4. If you are using heavy leather and want a sharper foldline, use the U or V cutting tool (*page 28*) and make a cut on the back of the leather.

5. Set your divider to 1/16″. Run it along the edges of pieces No. 1 and No. 2 where indicated on illustration 2 to make a guideline for your stitching punch (*page 29*). Now mark four dots in the corners of pieces No. 1 and No. 2 to indicate where your rivets will go.

6. Punch stitching holes (*page 29*). There should be the same number of holes on the No. 1 piece as on the No. 2 piece, since they are to be stitched together. You may end up with fewer holes punched on one piece than on the other. If this happens, simply center the side piece, at the bottom, with the bottom of the part of the bag on which it is to be sewn. This sounds a lot more complicated than it is. Just look at illustration 3 on which the lines are indicated.

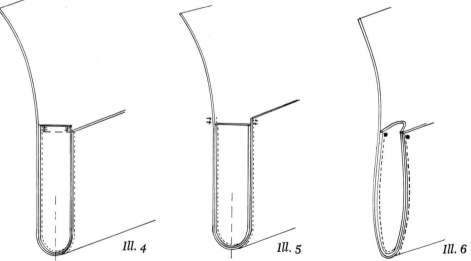

Ill. 4   *Ill. 5*   *Ill. 6*

7. Sew (*page 32*) your No. 1 and No. 2 pieces together, wrong side to wrong side. (*Ill. 4*)

8. Trim the sides so that they are the same length. (*Ill. 5*)

9. With your rotary punch, punch your rivet holes and insert rivets (*page 35*).

10. Finish the edges (*page 44*). Wax and stain, if you like, as shown in illustration 6.

NOTE CASE WITH STRAP / Easy

Cowhide, kip, heavy suede or latigo

1. Make your paper pattern (*page 23*) following the cutting lines for B on illustration 2. Tape to your leather.

2. Cut one No. 1 piece and mark the foldlines on the reverse side of your leather.

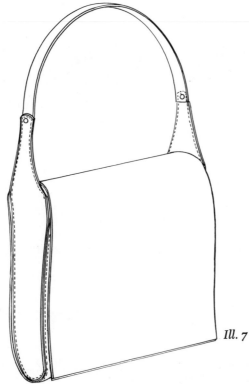

Ill. 7

3. Cut two full No. 2 pieces and one No. 3 piece for the strap. Mark the No. 2 and No. 3 pieces for rivets. Note that you will only need the one rivet at the end of piece No. 2.

4. If you are using heavy leather and want a sharper foldline, use the U or V cutting tool (*page 28*) and make a cut in the back of the leather.

5. Set your divider and mark and punch your leather as in steps 5 and 6 for the Note Case.

6. Sew the bag together as for the Note Case.

7. Sew the strap, No. 3 piece, to the side pieces as shown in illustrations 8 and 9.

8. With your rotary punch, punch rivet holes where the sides meet the strap. (*Ill. 8*) Insert rivets (*page 35*).

9. Finish the edges (*page 44*). Wax and stain, if you like.

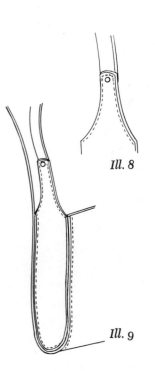

Ill. 8

Ill. 9

BALL BAG / Intermediate

Soft leather, suede or cabretta

PREPARING THE LEATHER

1. ·Make your paper pattern (*page 23*) according to illustration 11.
2. Tape pattern to leather.
3. Using heavy scissors, cut two No. 1 pieces; one No. 2 piece; one No. 3 piece; one No. 4 piece.

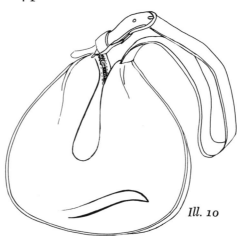

Ill. 10

4. Mark the foldlines on the wrong side of the leather.
5. Cut cording long enough to go around one No. 1 piece at the stitching line.
6. Cut a strip of leather as long as the cording and wide enough to go around it with a 3/8″ seam allowance.

TO ASSEMBLE

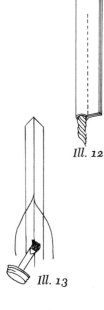

Ill. 12

Ill. 13

1. Cover the cording with the leather strip and stitch it as close to the cording as possible (*Ill. 12*) with a running stitch or by machine.
2. Fold the edges of your No. 3 piece, which will be your strap, to the middle and glue in place. (*Ill. 13*) You can use the same instructions for this strap as in Basic Tie Belt, page oo.
3. Fold in and glue the edges of the keeper, the No. 4 piece.
4. With your oblong punch, make a hole (*page 30*) for the buckle in the No. 3 piece (the buckle end of the strap), and glue in the edges as in step 2.
5. Place the buckle tongue in the hole of the No. 3 piece and fold the leather across the center. Stitch the keeper and the buckle in place

(*page 38*). Stitch only those stitches nearest the buckle (the row between the arrows as shown in illustration 14). Be sure to make seven stitches in this row. Slide the keeper in place.

6. Set the divider to 1/16″. Run it along the edges of both No. 1 pieces where indicated on the illustration to make a guideline for your stitching punch. Punch the holes (*page 29*).

7. Place the No. 1 pieces together, right side to right side, with a 3/8″ seam allowance of the cording placed between the seam allowances of the bag. Sew together. (*Ill. 15*)

8. Turn the bag right side out. Punch nine holes (*page 29*) for stitches, 1 1/2″ from the top edge of each side of the bag. The fifth

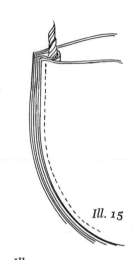

Ill. 14

Ill. 15

Ill. 11

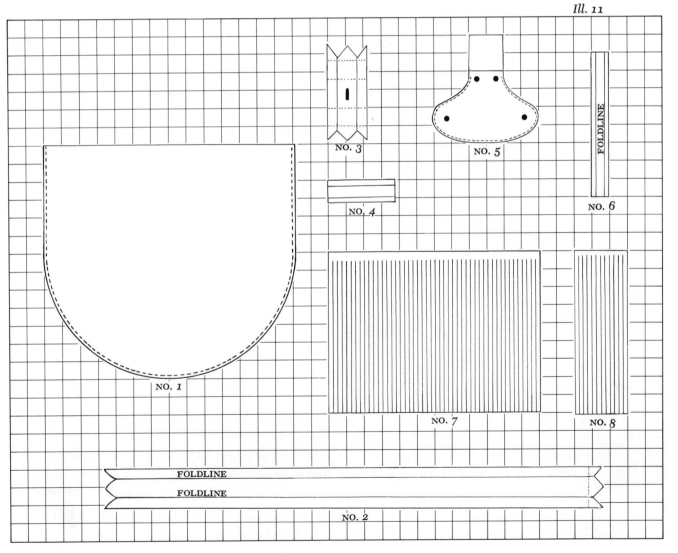

NO. 3

NO. 5

FOLDLINE

NO. 6

NO. 4

NO. 1

NO. 7

NO. 8

FOLDLINE

FOLDLINE

NO. 2

stitch should go through the cording. (*Ill. 16*) Place the strap end in place at the side of the top edge of the bag. (*Ill. 17*) Punch four holes vertically, 1 1/8″ to each side of the cording as in illustration 16. Now punch seven holes on the strap piece, as indicated on the No. 2 piece.

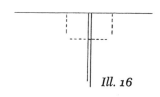

Ill. 16

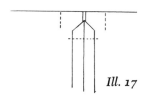

Ill. 17

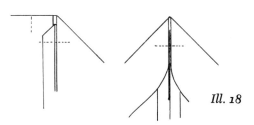

Ill. 18

9. Fold the top edge of the bag into the cording so that it goes down to form a V around the end of the strap and cording. Stitch in place. (*Ill. 18*) Turn right side out. (*Ill. 19*) The strap should be centered on the cording if all went well. Repeat this whole process, putting the buckle end in place, on the top edge of the other side of the bag, and sew the seven stitches in the bottom row. (*Ill. 14*)

10. Put your zipper in place at the top of the bag as shown in illustration 20 and topstitch it in place.

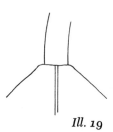

Ill. 19

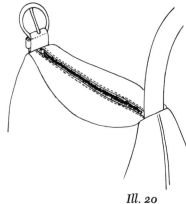

Ill. 20

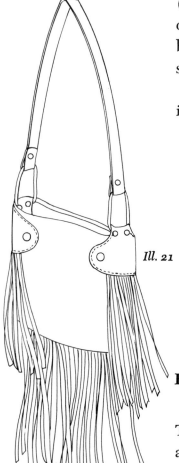

Ill. 21

FRINGED BAG / ADVANCED

Soft leather, suede, or cabretta

This bag has the same round body as the one before. Long fringe is added for decoration and the corners are made differently. However, you should use the same basic pattern as for the Ball Bag.

PREPARING THE LEATHER

1. Make your pattern (*page 23*) according to illustration 11 and tape it to the leather.

2. With scissors, cut out two No. 1 pieces; one No. 2 piece; two No. 5 pieces; two No. 6 pieces; one No. 7 piece; two No. 8 pieces.

3. Mark the fold and stitching lines, as well as where the rivets should go.

4. For the bottom fringe, take the No. 7 piece and cut even strips into it, making sure to leave about 1/2″ uncut along the top of the piece to hold the fringe together. Cut both No. 8 pieces in the same manner for the side fringe. (For more information about fringe, see page 125.)

TO ASSEMBLE

1. Sew the two No. 1 pieces together right side to right side, placing the uncut edge of the fringe between the two pieces. (*Ill. 22*) If you aren't using a machine, set your divider for 3/8″ and run it along both No. 1 pieces and the top of the No. 7 piece. Punch holes with your prong (*page 29*) and stitch through all three pieces by hand. Otherwise, stitch through the pieces by machine.

2. Turn the bag right side out. Turn the top edge 3/8″ under and glue. (*Ill. 23, arrow*) Stitch, if you like.

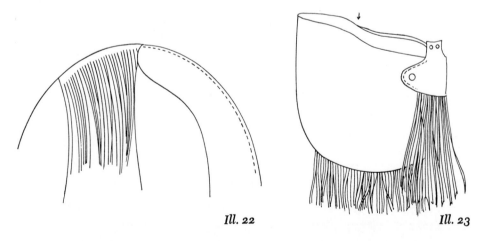

Ill. 22   *Ill. 23*

3. Place your two No. 5 pieces at each end of the bag, so that the bottom of the piece is 3 3/4″ down from the top. Place the fringe between the bag and the No. 5 piece with the center of the fringe at

Ill. 24

the side seam. Glue the No. 5 pieces down, catching the fringe in place, and then punch your holes through all three pieces. Stitch as in illustration 23. Attach lower rivets (*page 35*) as seen in illustration.

4. Fold to the center and glue in place the No. 2 piece (the strap) and the No. 6 piece (the strap extension). Stitch the ends of the No. 6 pieces together to form a loop. Fold the tops of these anchor pieces over the loops and rivet. (*Ill. 24*)

5. Fold the strap around the loops and rivet it in place. (*Ill. 24*)

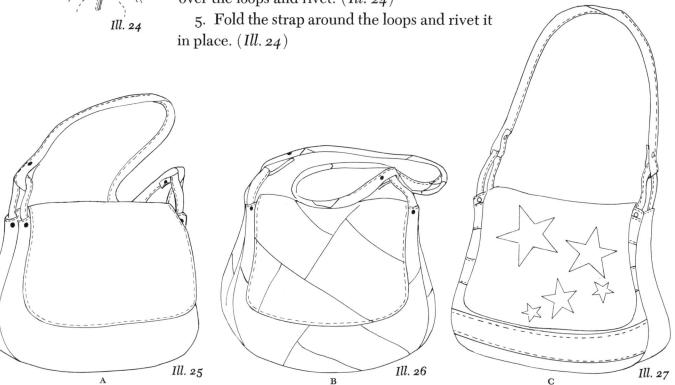

A   *Ill. 25*   B   *Ill. 26*   C   *Ill. 27*

SHOULDER BAGS—A. PLAIN B. QUILTED C. DECORATED / Intermediate

Soft leather, suede or cabretta

These three bags are alike except for the added quilting and decorating on bags B and C. Do the quilting and decorating before assembling the bags. The quilting on bag B is made up of overlapped leather scraps. You may either zigzag or straight-stitch them together. (*Ill. 28*) Then cut your pattern as if it were one solid piece. I made bag C in red, white and blue. The sides, straps and strap holders in white, the front and back in white with red stripes (*Ill. 29*) and the flap in blue backed with white.

PREPARING THE LEATHER

1. Cut out your pattern pieces (*page 23*) according to illustration 30 and tape them to the leather. With scissors, cut out the pieces, allowing a 3/8″ seam allowance for each piece.

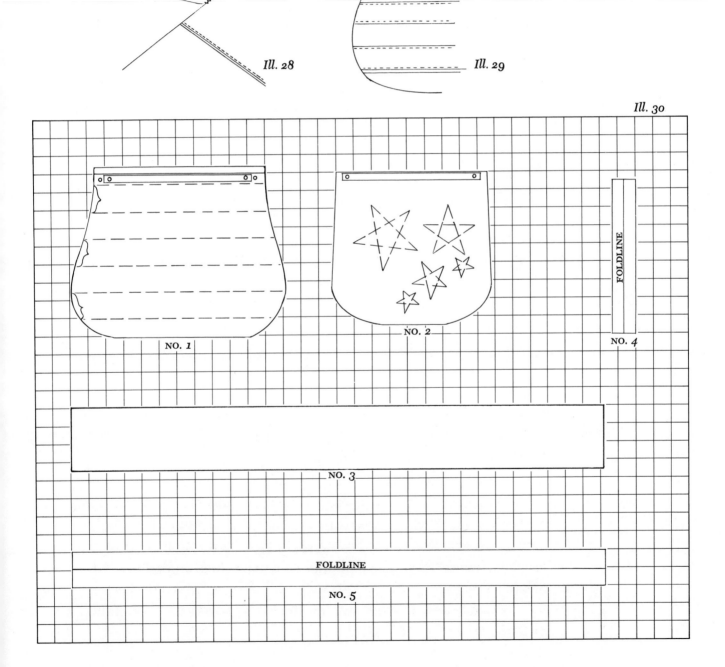

Ill. 28

Ill. 29

Ill. 30

NO. 1

NO. 2

FOLDLINE
NO. 4

NO. 3

FOLDLINE
NO. 5

2. Cut two No. 1 pieces and one No. 2 piece for bags A and B. For bag C cut two No. 1 pieces in white, and two No. 2 pieces, one in white (with a 3/8″ seam allowance trimmed off all around except the top) and one in blue.

4. For bag C, draw any size stars you like on brown paper for a pattern. Tape the paper to your blue piece and cut the stars out with an Exacto knife. (*Ill. 31*) Then glue the blue piece over the white No. 2 piece.

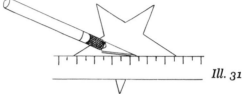

Ill. 31

5. Cut one No. 3 piece; two No. 4 pieces; one No. 5 piece.
6. Mark your leather for rivets, as indicated on the pattern.

TO ASSEMBLE

1. The No. 3 piece winds around your bag to form the bottom and sides. Sew your two No. 1 pieces to the No. 3 piece with right sides together. (*Ill. 32*)
2. Turn the 3/8″ seam allowance of pieces No. 1 down at the top of the bag. Glue it. Stitch it, if you like.

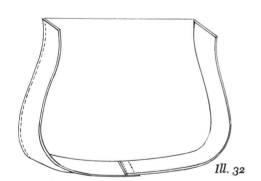

Ill. 32

Ill. 33

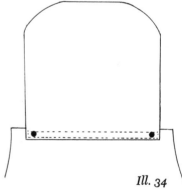

Ill. 34

3. Turn back the seam allowance on the flap, the No. 2 piece, except for the top which will be attached to the bag. Glue and stitch the hem down, easing in the rounded corners. (*Ill. 33*) On bag C, the starred top can be left unstitched. The blue edge should be glued around the white piece.

4. Using two rows of stitches, sew the No. 2 piece to the back of the bag on the outside. (*Ill. 34*)

5. Double the No. 4 and 5 pieces. Glue them (*page 40*) and stitch 1/16″ from the raw edge. (*Ill. 35*)

6. Place the ends of your No. 4 pieces, the strap extensions, on each side of the bag. (*Ill. 36*) Punch holes in the bag and strap extensions and rivet them in place.

7. Rivet the No. 5 piece, the strap, around these extensions.

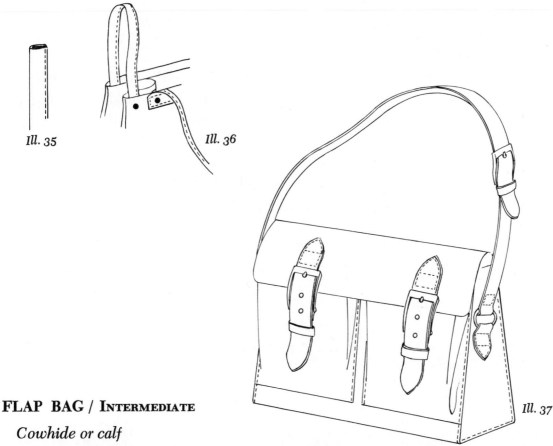

Ill. 35

Ill. 36

Ill. 37

FLAP BAG / Intermediate

Cowhide or calf

This bag and the following one are from the same basic pattern. They are both easy to make, but take some patience because the leather is heavy and they need a good deal of pounding and stitching.

PREPARING THE LEATHER

1. Cut out your pattern pieces (*page 23*) according to illustration 38 and tape them to your leather.

2. With your utility knife against a metal edge, cut out one No. 1 piece; two No. 2 pieces (cutting them off for this bag on the line marked for bag A); two No. 3 pieces.

3. Cut nine No. 5 pieces for straps (*page 26*) to the dimensions below:

> Two straps 30" × 1 1/4"
> One strap 26 1/2" × 1 1/4"
> Two flap straps 7 1/2" × 1 1/4"
> Two side anchors for straps 3 1/4" × 1 1/4"
> Two straps for pocket buckles 5" × 1 1/4"

4. Now cut three No. 6 belt keepers 3 1/2" × 1/2"

TO ASSEMBLE

1. The No. 3 pieces are your pockets. Shape the ends of your two 5 × 1 1/4" straps to match the pattern. Attach the buckles to each strap (*page 38*). Now attach the No. 6 pieces, the keepers. Rivet these straps, with the keepers, in place on the pockets. (*Ill. 39*)

2. Shape the two 7 1/2" × 1 1/4" straps to fit on the flap of the No. 1 piece where shown in illustration 40. Glue these in place. Punch with your stitching punch and stitch in place.

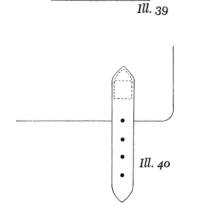

Ill. 39

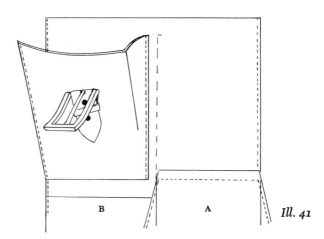

Ill. 40

B   A   *Ill. 41*

3. Punch stitching holes all the way around the No. 1 piece, except for the top and flap, 1/16" from the edge. Punch holes in front for the pockets indicated by the dotted line on the pattern.

4. Punch holes on the bottom foldline of your No. 3 piece (the pockets) and along each side edge. Don't punch holes on the top. Wet the pockets and fold them along the foldlines.

5. Sew (*page 32*) the pockets to the bottom front of the bag, right side to right side. (*Ill. 41, a*)

6. Now, turn the pockets up and stitch the center seam of each pocket in place. (*Ill. 41, b*)

7. Punch holes on three sides of your No. 2 pieces, 1/16″ from the edge, but not on the top.

Ill. 38

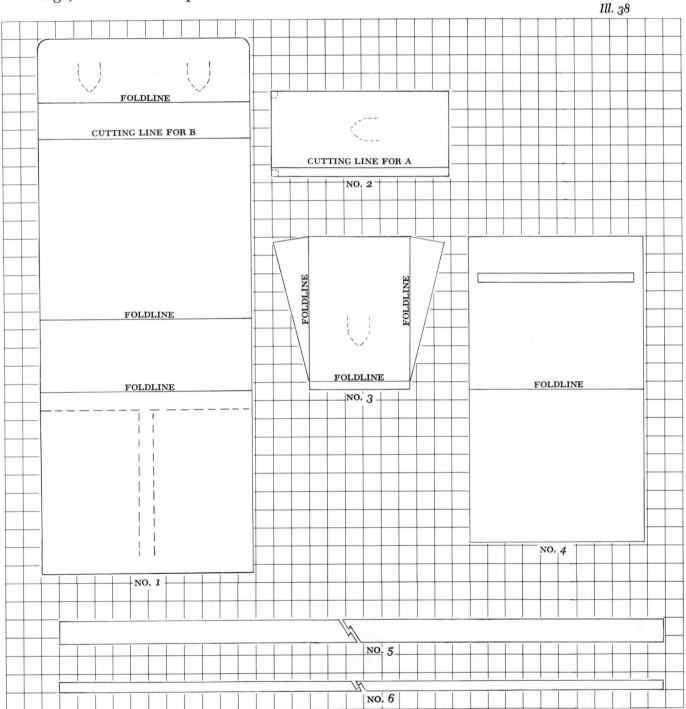

8. Shape the 3 1/4″ × 1 1/4″ side anchors for straps and punch. Choose two rings of appropriate size and stitch in place. Sew these anchor straps to both No. 2 pieces. (*Ill. 42*)

9. Sew the No. 2 pieces to the body of the bag. Make sure to catch the pockets in the side seams. (*Ill. 43*)

10. The longer strap on this bag is now put together. Pull one of the 30″ × 1 1/4″ straps through the ring (*Ill. 42*), lining up both ends of the strap. Glue together.

11. Take the other 30″ × 1 1/4″ strap. Punch an oblong hole in it 13 1/4″ from one end. Slide the buckle into the strap, with keeper in place, and attach buckle (*page 38*). Put the longer end of the strap through the other ring and glue and stitch in place. (*Ill. 44*)

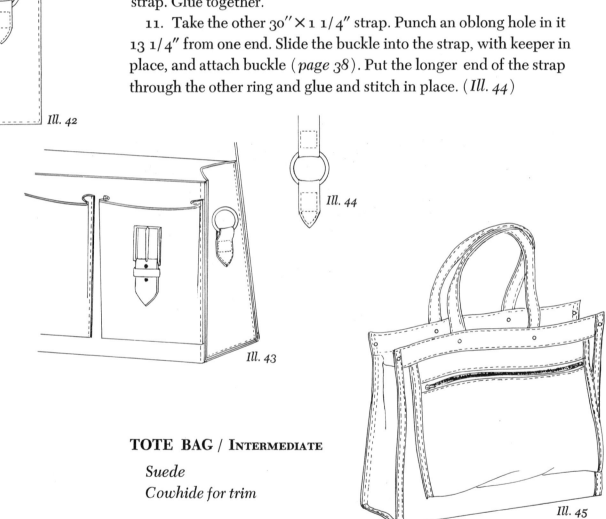

Ill. 42

Ill. 44

Ill. 43

TOTE BAG / INTERMEDIATE

Suede
Cowhide for trim

PREPARING THE LEATHER

1. Cut out the pattern pieces (*page 23*) according to illustration 38, using the pattern lines for B, and tape them to your leather.

2. With scissors, cut from the suede: one No. 1 piece, up to the line marked в; two No. 2 pieces, cutting off two corners 3/8″ as marked by

Ill. 45

the dotted line; one No. 4 piece, cutting out the 10″ slot marked for the 10″ zipper and six No. 5 pieces out of cowhide to the dimensions below:

Four straps 16″ × 1 1/4″

Two straps 12″ × 1 1/4″

3. Cut from the cowhide four No. 6 pieces for the trim: two pieces 25″ × 1 1/2″ and two pieces 9″ × 1/2″.

TO ASSEMBLE

1. Put the zipper in the slot on the No. 4 piece. Glue it to the wrong side of the leather. Punch holes around the zipper and topstitch. (*Ill. 46*)

2. Fold the No. 4 piece on the foldine. Glue the side edges together to make a pocket.

3. Skive (*page 27*) one end of each of the 9″ × 1/2″ cowhide pieces.

4. Glue the trim to the side of the pocket piece, turning the skived end 1/2″ under the bottom edge of the pocket. (*Ill. 46*) Run your divider along the trim for a guideline for the stitching punch (*page 29*) to make two lines—one 1/8″ from the edge and the other 3/8″ from the edge. Punch and stitch (*page 29*) as shown in illustration 46.

5. Glue the pocket to the No. 1 piece, centering it 1/2″ from the top. (*Ill. 47*) Fold the No. 1 piece on the foldlines.

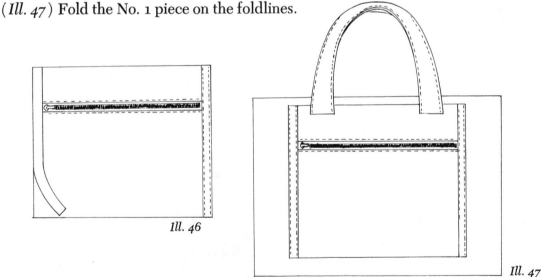

Ill. 46

Ill. 47

6. Glue two of the 16″ × 1 1/4″ No. 5 pieces together for each handle. Punch stitching holes 1/8″ from the edge and stitch all around.

7. Center the handle straps on both the front and back side of the No. 1 pieces and 1″ down from the top. Glue. (*Ill. 47*)

8. Glue the two 12″ × 1 1/4″ No. 5 pieces across the top of the bag on each side and over the handle. Glue the two 25″ × 1/2″ No. 6 pieces down both sides for the front of the bag. (*Ill. 48*)

9. Punch stitching holes 1/8″ and 3/8″ from the edges of the side trim and 1/8″ from both edges of the trim on the top. (*Ill. 48*) Stitch the top edges with the handles between the bag and trim.

10. Turn in the side edges of the No. 2 piece 1/2″ and glue. (*Ill. 49*) Now punch the same number of holes in the No. 2 pieces, in two rows: 1/8″ and 3/8″ from the outer edges. (*Ill. 50*)

11. Center the side pieces and stitch in place (*page 32*).

12. Punch holes and put in rivets where the handles meet the bag and in the four corners.

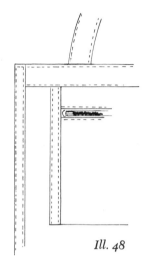

Ill. 48

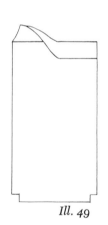

Ill. 49

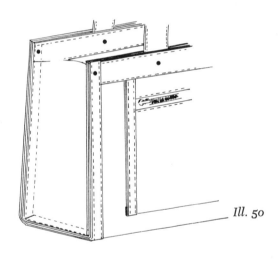

Ill. 50

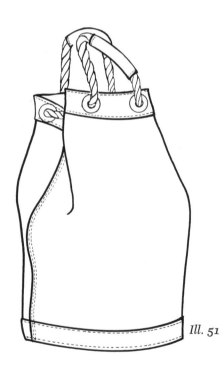

Ill. 51

DUFFEL BAG / Intermediate

Suede or kip
Cowhide for trim

Instructions are given here for a nice-looking utilitarian duffel bag. You can use any kind of rope you like, as long as it fits through a size 5 grommet. Cut it to the handle length you like. You can also make this same bag a little smaller and shorter for a dress-up bag, using a chain for a handle, instead of rope.

PREPARING THE LEATHER

1. Cut out your pattern pieces (*page 23*) according to illustration 52 and tape them to your leather.

2. With your utility knife against a metal square, cut out of the suede or kip two No. 1 pieces and one No. 2 piece; out of the cowhide, cut four No. 3 pieces and two No. 4 pieces 5″ × 1 3/4″.

Ill. 52

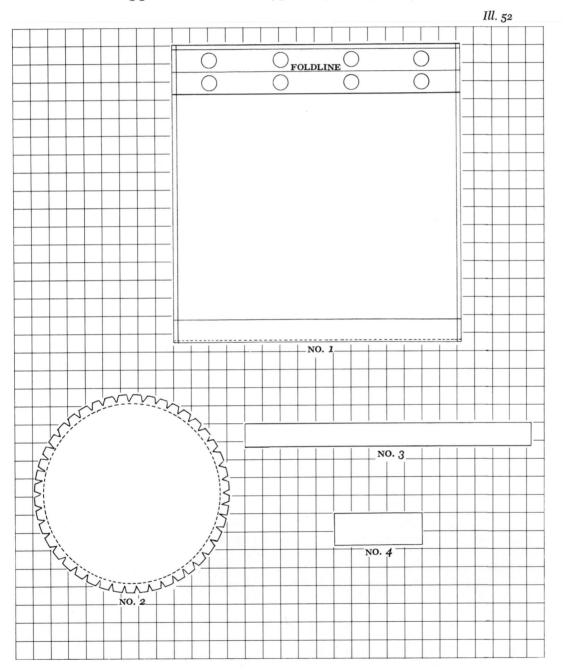

TO ASSEMBLE

1. Glue the four No. 3 pieces, the trim, to the top and bottom of both No. 1 pieces. The top trim pieces are glued at the foldline; the bottom trim pieces are aligned with the bottom of piece No. 1 (*Ill. 53*)

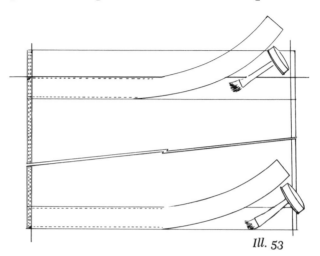

Ill. 53

2. Set your divider to 1/8″ and run it along each side of the trim. Punch the holes for stitching (*Ill. 53*)

3. Punch stitching holes for the side seams 1/16″ and 3/16″ from the edge. These seams are flat fell seams and will overlap 1/4″. (*Ill. 54*) Stitch the side seams to form a big tube.

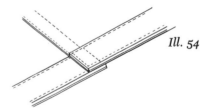

Ill. 54

4. Stitch the two rows of the top trim and the top row of the bottom trim.

5. Fold the top of the bag under 1 1/2″ and glue in place.

6. Punch stitching holes on the circular bottom of the No. 2 piece. (*Ill. 52*) Wet this piece and turn up the edges along the stitching line.

7. Stitch the No. 2 piece to the bottom of the bag, through the trim. (*Ill. 55*)

8. Punch eight holes around the top trim for size 5 grommets, and set the grommets according to instructions on page 36. (*Ill. 56*)

9. Put your piece of rope through all the holes and sew the ends together.

10. Punch stitching holes around the edges of your No. 4 pieces.

11. Place No. 4 pieces around the rope and stitch along top edges.

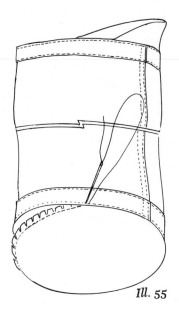

Ill. 55

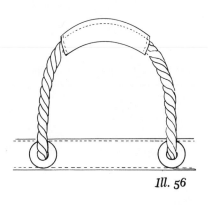

Ill. 56

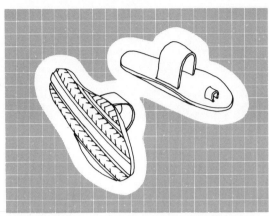

Sandals

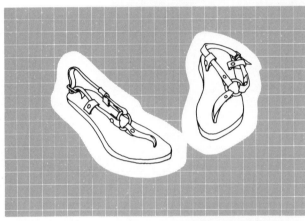

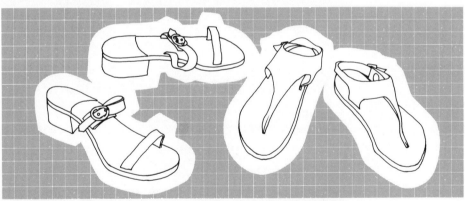

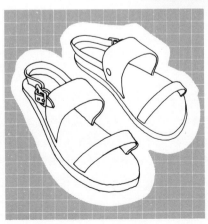

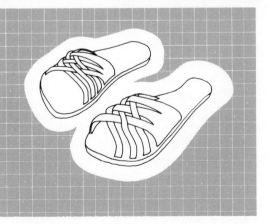

Sandals are airy, fashionable and very good for your feet. They are easy to make, and compared to what they cost in shoe stores, they are also very inexpensive to do yourself. Most important, the sandals you make yourself are custom-made to your own foot.

All sandals consist of top and bottom soles and straps. They can be made with heels or without, heavy and rugged or light and dainty, completely of leather or with a rubber sole. (Recyclers take note: old automobile tires can be cut into good bottom soles, as they are in Morocco and Greece and other economy-minded places.)

Sandals can be glued and then nailed (cobbled), or glued, nailed, and then stitched. Stitched sandals wear better, nailed sandals look dressier. Probably, if you want stitched sandals, you should get your shoemaker to do the job for you, since it is very hard work.

You can sand your sandals by hand or you can take them to your friendly neighborhood shoe repairman to do this job also. As you can imagine, he's a good man to make friends with.

Tools and Materials for Sandal Making

The following is a list of tools that you will need to make sandals. The list is quite complete, and you shouldn't run out and buy all these things before you begin. I have marked the tools you really need with an asterisk but read the instructions very carefully before you begin making the sandals you decide on to see what you will need for that particular job.

TOOLS

*Utility or cobblers' knife
*Metal square
*Four-prong punch
*Oblong drive punch—Buy a sturdy steel punch, in the 5/8″ size. When the hole has to be longer for wider straps, you can move the punch along the first hole and punch again. Don't invest in a really expensive punch which comes in larger sizes (*page 13*).

*Rawhide maul
*Metal hammer or sole hammer
*Skife knife
*Electric motor—flat and drum sanding wheel with coarse sandpaper; felt or lapping wheel for polishing.
*Rotary punch
*V-edge beveler
*Round driver punch
*Stump or endgrain block

*Cutting board
*Needles
*Scissors
*Adjustable groover
Ruffer
Pliers
Hand drill—useful for high-heeled sandals.
Hardwood wheel (Slick)
Strap cutter (Draw gauge)
Landis sole cutter

MATERIALS

Leather for sandal straps and tops—oil- or chrome-tanned cowhide; kips are fine for fitted tops.

Leather for bottom soles—10- or 11-iron prime flexible sole for heavy sandals; 6-iron prime for lighter ones.

Rubber for bottom soles—of equal thickness as sole leather (possibly from an old tire).

Leather for top soles—10 or 11 oz. flexible belting.

Nails—1/2", 3/8" and 5/8"

clinching nails for cobbling (brass nails won't rust); 6/8" threaded wood heel nails for high heels.

Screws—7/8" #4 screws for high heels.

Wax—beeswax or cake wax.

Rivets

Metal arches—for high-heeled sandals.

Buckles—to fit the straps.

Coarse sandpaper—for hand-sanding.

Brass rings—for certain sandals.

Sandal Soles

You can make soles that fit your foot exactly by tracing around your feet to make a pattern. Soles come in two parts, the top and bottom sole. Of course you must make them to fit two different feet, your left foot and your right foot. The instructions for making soles for the

Flat Sandal are basic to all flat sandals. Separate directions will be given for high-heel soles and variations of the flat sole with the individual project.

If you want a Village-style, heavy-soled sandal, the top sole should be 10- or 11-oz.-thick top, flexible belting cowhide. If the top sole is made from cowhide and not sole leather, it will more quickly conform to the foot, because it is softer.

The bottom sole is made of 10- or 11-iron prime flexible sole leather. Rubber can be used for the bottom sole and is also sold in irons. If a lighter sole is desired, use 5- or 6-iron bottom sole.

Sandal Tops

Sandal tops can be made of straps or of a piece of leather fitted to your foot. When fitting tops, remember that your feet should be able to move freely, since they bend when you walk.

Straps can be placed in several places (*Ill. 1*): 1) in front or in back of the large joint of your big toe; 2) in front or in back of the joint on your smallest toe; 3) at the highest point of your arch, at the instep, and across from this point; and 4) between your big toe and the toe next to it, for thong sandals.

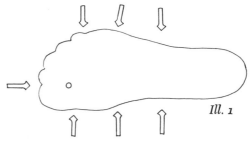

Ill. 1

To make patterns for a specific strap you want, get some heavy brown paper. Fold it to the width of the strap you desire. You can experiment with various widths or make combinations of wide and narrow straps, but make sure to settle on a width you can buy a buckle to fit. Standard buckle sizes are 3/8″, 1/2″, 5/8″, 3/4″,

7/8″, 1″ or 1 1/4″. Wrap these patterns around your foot (*Ill. 2*) until you get the effect you want. Then you are ready to cut out your leather.

Fitted tops are generally made of soft leather—such as kip or heavy suede—and are cut out and molded to your foot. To make a pattern for a fitted top, use a piece of fabric cut into a rectangle 2″ longer than your toe in front and 4″ longer than your heel in back. (*Ill. 3*) Cut down the center of this fabric somewhat less than halfway. Pull the ends of the fabric back so that the uncut part fits snugly over your instep. (It is nice if you can get a friend to help you with this tricky job).

Fit the fabric on your foot and, with a felt-tip pen, outline on the fabric the shape of sandal top you want. Cut this shape out and try it on. Modify the fabric if it doesn't fit properly. Now, tape the fabric pattern onto heavy brown paper and cut out the shape.

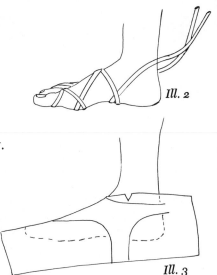

Ill. 2

Ill. 3

FLAT SANDAL / Easy

This sandal can be made for men, women or children. These instructions are for the flat sandal (*Ill. 4*), but you can also make it with a heel. (*Ill. 5*)

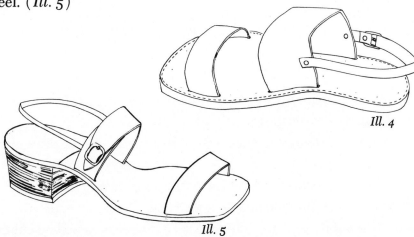

Ill. 4

Ill. 5

TO MAKE THE SOLES

The instructions for making these patterns for soles can be used for all flat-soled sandals and will be referred to in the other projects.

1. The shape of your foot determines the sole's shape. Take a piece of cardboard, the weight of shirt cardboard. Stand on it squarely. Hold a pen at 90° angle to one foot and carefully trace around it onto the cardboard. (*Ill. 6*) Don't let your pen make an undercut line or cut out away from your foot. (*Dotted lines in Ill. 7*) Since almost everybody's feet are slightly different in size, it's safest to make a separate pattern for your other foot in the same way. Mark the high point of your arch on the pattern. (*Ill. 8*) This mark is made both for installing a leather arch if you want one, and also to help you with the location of your straps. If your arch is flat, make sure your foot outline doesn't cut in at the arch point, but goes quite straight instead. If you are making thong sandals, before you get off the cardboard, mark the deepest point between your big toe and the toe next to it. Now, take your feet off the cardboard.

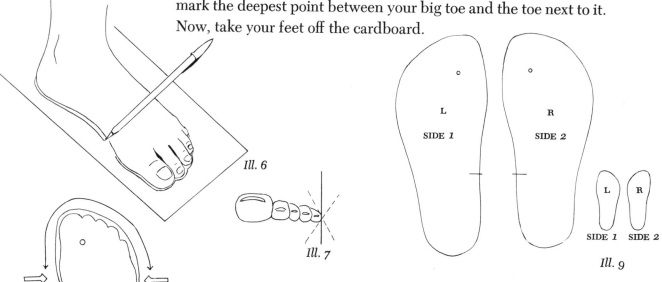

Ill. 6

Ill. 7

Ill. 8

Ill. 9

2. Trace the line around your toes on the cardboard that is indicated by the arrows in illustration 8. This line should be 1/4″ from your footprint. For the rest of the pattern, the line should be drawn 1/8″ from your footprint.

3. To avoid confusion, cut the pattern for the top sole of your right foot first, following the outside line. Then, *reverse the pattern* and cut the bottom sole for your right foot. (These patterns will be cut out of different leathers, as the following instructions make clear.) Follow the same process for your left foot, cutting the top sole, then reversing the pattern and cutting the bottom sole. Always mark the pattern pieces right and left, side 1 and side 2. (*Ill. 9*)

4. Place the pattern for your right foot on a piece of *top* sole leather, placed right side up. Mark the leather around the cardboard pattern with an awl. Using a utility knife or a cobbler's knife, cut 1/4″ away from your awl mark all the way around the pattern. (*Ill. 10, line* A) This gives you an allowance of extra leather to insure against error and so that your foot doesn't hang out over the sole. Pull the knife toward you and cut as you pull it. (*Ill. 10*) It will probably be necessary to make a few cuts to get through the leather unless you are very strong.

5. Now reverse the pattern for the right foot and place it on a piece of *bottom* sole leather which is lying *right side up* on your cutting surface. Make sure to use side 2 of the pattern. Now mark around the cardboard pattern with an awl. With your knife, cut 1/4″ away from your awl mark. (*Ill. 10*)

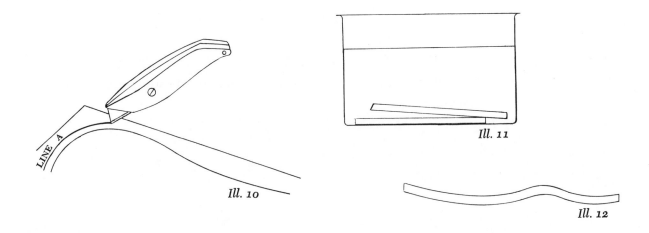

LINE A

Ill. 10

Ill. 11

Ill. 12

6. Follow the same process for cutting the top and bottom soles of your left foot.

7. Fill a clean, rustproof container with water. Immerse all the sole pieces in the water for about half an hour. (*Ill. 11*) Now take the soles out and let them dry until there is no apparent moisture on them. Place them on the bottoms of your feet and press them with your hands to shape them to the curves of your feet. If you want an arch in the soles, pull the leather up at your arch mark and turn up the heel and toe slightly. (*Ill. 12*) Shape the bottom soles to fit the top soles and let the soles dry out away from direct heat. They will dry in shape.

TO MAKE THE TOPS

The strap patterns shown in illustration 4 and indicated below are the right length for medium-size feet:

12″ long arch strap, 2″ wide
10″ long toe strap, 1″ wide
14″ heel strap, 5/8″ wide
4″ heel strap (buckle end), 5/8″ wide

Of course, test the length you need for your own personal foot by trying out a paper pattern for the straps and adding an extra inch or so for insurance. (If you're making sandals for a child, you'll have to make narrower straps.)

1. Make the patterns for the two arch straps, 2″ wide and the length you need. These straps have to go over the arch, through the sole, and then meet underneath. Be sure to make them long enough.

2. Now make the patterns for two toe straps, 1″ wide and the length you need, and for the heel straps. Two of these straps should be 5/8″ wide and long enough so they will go around your heel and end just beyond your ankle bone. The other two should be 5/8″ wide and long enough to hold the buckle, which means allowing an extra inch or so.

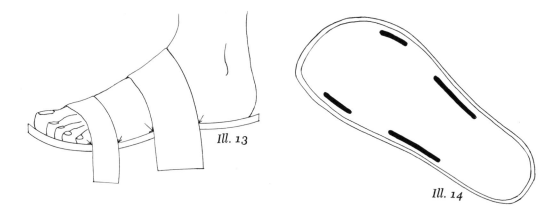

Ill. 13

Ill. 14

3. Tape your paper strap patterns on the leather and cut the straps with a utility knife (*page 24*), using a metal square for a guide. If you have a draw gauge, you can use that to cut the straps (*page 26*). Finish the edges of your straps (*page 44*). If you want to stain your straps, do so now, but remember that natural straps will darken from contact with your skin.

ASSEMBLING THE SANDAL

1. Stand on the top soles. Place the straps across your feet where you want them to fall. (*Ill. 13*) Mark with an awl on your top sole the points where the straps meet the sole. The arrow marks in illustration 13 give you the area for and width of the straps. Now move the straps 1/4″ inside your awl line and mark your leather for punching. (*Ill. 14*)

2. Place these top soles on an endgrain block or stump. With an oblong punch, make a hole (*page 30*) for each sandal strap as you have marked them (*Ill. 14*), moving the punch along to make the hole long enough to fit the straps into. Be careful not to punch too near the edge, because then you won't be able to stitch the sandals. The straps should look as though they come from under the foot.

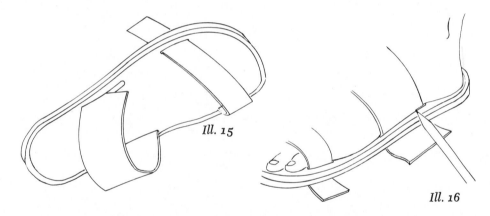

Ill. 15

Ill. 16

3. Put your arch straps and toe straps through the proper holes, pulling them from underneath with pliers if necessary. (*Ill. 15*) Put your feet on the top sole and pull the straps around your foot for a good snug fit. Center your feet on the top sole, put your weight on it, and pull again. It is good to have someone else do the pulling for you so that you can maintain your weight firmly on the sandals. The straps should feel pretty tight at this point because they will stretch with wear. Make sure, while you're doing this fitting, that your heel is within the awl line indicating the outline of your foot. With a pen, mark the point on the straps where they will go through the holes in the top soles. (*Ill. 16*) If you are making thong sandals, punch the thong holes and pull the straps through. Mark where your thong goes between your big toe and the toe next to it on the top sole.

4. Pull the straps under the top soles so that they meet neatly underneath. (*Ill. 17*) Make sure the straps are in the proper position for the top of the sandal. Cut off any excess so that the straps just meet underneath, with no overlap. (*Ill. 18, cross section*)

5. Glue the straps in place underneath the top sole and if you have a motor with a sanding wheel, sand some of the bulk away (the sanded area is shown by the dark line in illustration 18). If you have no motor, remove some of the bulk where the straps meet under the sole at the toe and arch (*Ill. 19A*) with an adjustable groover. Make sure not to make these areas so thin that the straps pull through the top of the sandals. If you wish, you can cross-stitch them in place as in illustration 19B to make them especially secure. Remember on all gluing to apply glue to both surfaces, and let the glue become tacky before tapping the surfaces together.

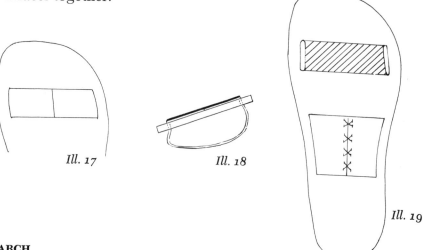

Ill. 17   *Ill. 18*

Ill. 19

THE ARCH

1. If your foot has a particularly high instep, you may want to place an arch under the top sole. Cut the arch out of a thick piece of rubber or leather (10 or 12 irons) in the shape indicated in illustration 20. The center of the arch should fall two-thirds of the way back on the sandal sole. (*Profile of arch at edge beside sole, Ill. 20*) The high point of the arch should meet the high point you have marked on your sandals. The arch should taper away from its highest point, going down all the way around, like a mountain slope, as shown by the arrows in illustration 20. You can skive the arch (*page 27*) with a skife knife to get this effect or sand it if you have a motor. For faster sanding with a motor, place a wooden block behind the arch.

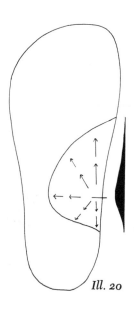

Ill. 20

HEEL STRAPS

1. Try on your sandal top and top sole. Bring the heel straps around your heel to meet the arch straps, marking the points on your arch straps where the heel straps feel most comfortable. Rivet (*page 35*) the short heel straps which will fall on the outside of your foot and hold the buckle to the arch straps. (*Ill. 21*) Rivet the long heel straps to the parts of the arch straps which are on the inside of your foot, opposite the ones you've just placed. Attach buckles (*page 38*) to the short heel straps. With a rotary punch (*page 30*) make holes on the long heel straps with which to fasten the buckle. The holes should be 3/8″ apart and the size of the buckle's tongue.

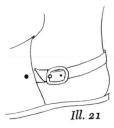

Ill. 21

GLUING THE SOLES TOGETHER

1. The wrong sides of the top and bottom soles should be ruffed with a ruffer, a razor, or a sharp fork before gluing so that the glue will hold. (*Ill. 22*)

2. Apply glue to both ruffed soles on each sandal. (*Ill. 23*) Allow the glue to get tacky and then put the soles together. Start at the toe and work down toward the heel as you cement. (*Ill. 24*) Place the sandals, top sole down, on a smooth surface and, working on the bottom sole, tap the soles firmly all around the edge, with overlapping taps. (*Ill. 25*) Use a sole hammer or a metal hammer with a slightly curved head.

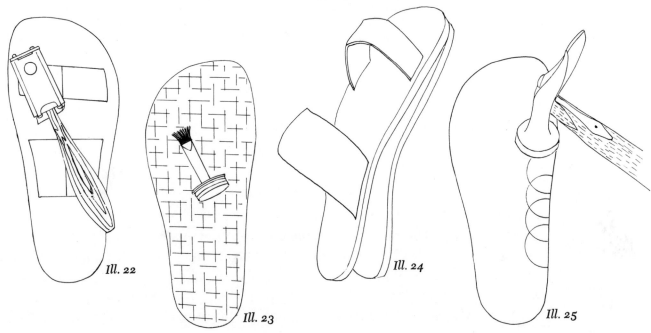

Ill. 22

Ill. 23

Ill. 24

Ill. 25

STITCHING AND COBBLING

If you want stitched sandals, you will have to send them to a shoemaker, who will do the job on his machine. Most shoemakers will sand and stitch your sandals for a relatively small fee. One of Greenwich Village's best sandal makers used to have his stitching done by a shoe repair shop next door to him. When the sandal maker finally got big enough, he bought out the shop. The shoemaker's machine is adjustable, so you can ask for a length of stitch which appeals to you. For cobbled sandals, you can do the cobbling (nailing) yourself.

If your sandals are to be stitched, before taking them to the shoemaker, fit the arch to your foot and to the bottom of the bottom sole of the sandal. But do not glue it in place, because the shoemaker will not be able to stitch through three thicknesses of leather. Now refit the sandals for a final trimming of the soles and cleaning up. (The arch may make the sandal slightly shorter.) With either a utility knife or a cobbler's knife, trim your sandals. Unless you are very strong, a utility knife is better to use than a cobbler's knife. Hold your knife at right angles to the sole. Don't let the knife cut in too far. (Ill. 26 is a cross section of the proper cut to be made.) Keep your straps well out of the way when trimming the soles. Now they are ready for stitching.

When you get your sandals back from the shoemaker, you will glue the arch to the bottom of the bottom sole. (*Ill. 27*) Use your ruffer on

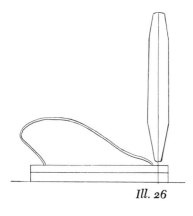

Ill. 26

Ill. 27

the areas of the arch and sole that will be glued together; glue the arch in place. (*Ill. 28*) Of course, the shoemaker can trim your sandals and glue the arch in place for you.

If you are going to sand and cobble the sandals yourself, however, you can attach the arch to the bottom of the bottom sole or between the top and bottom soles. Fit the arch to your foot and mark its outline on your leather where it is to be glued. Refit the sandals for a final trimming of the soles and cleaning up as above. Glue the arch in place.

To sand, place a flat sanding disk of coarse sandpaper on your motor. Always work below the center of the wheel. A view looking toward the wheel is shown in illustration 29. Hold the straps well away from the

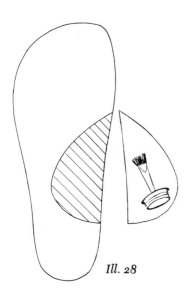

Ill. 28

motor's wheel. Sand the sides of your soles, always keeping the sandals moving at right angles to the wheel. Don't sand the indented areas, the arches and across from the arches with the flat disk. Instead, use a drum sander for this area. (*Ill. 30*) You can also do this sanding work by hand by wrapping coarse sandpaper around a stick and holding the sandal against a firm surface. (*Ill. 31*) Or use a coarse file or rasp.

Soles should now be cobbled with cobbling nails placed all around the soles and through the straps where they run through the soles. Cobbling nails have a thin tip and almost no head. They should be slightly longer than your sole is thick. Place your sandals on a metal

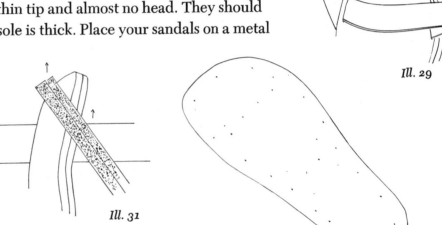

Ill. 29

Ill. 30   *Ill. 31*

Ill. 32

surface, with the bottom of the soles facing up. If you have no metal surface available, an old spatula placed on a firm flat surface will do. Nails should be spaced about 1″ apart all around the edge and through the straps to hold them firmly in place. (*Ill. 32*) Hit each nail with the hammer so that the nail penetrates the sole, hits the metal, and is bent back into the sole, locking itself in place. (*Ill. 33*) Even if your sandals are going to be stitched by the shoemaker, you can, if you like, cobble them yourself after stitching, placing the nails 2″ apart instead of 1″. *Do* cobble the straps in place in every case.

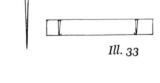

Ill. 33

Ill. 34

Ill. 35

FINISHING THE EDGES

1. Finish the edges of the soles (*page 44*) with a V-edged beveler. (*Ill. 34*) Stain the edges if you like (*Ill. 35*) and rub them with either beeswax or brown or black cake wax. If you have a motor, you can

polish the edges with a felt wheel or you can use a soft cloth. You can wax the edges by applying the wax directly to the area of the wheel shown in illustration 36. The friction of the wheel against the sandal heats the wax and helps it to penetrate further than does hand waxing. Wax has a nice dull sheen that is weatherproof. Don't use a shiny glazed finish. It will crack and come off.

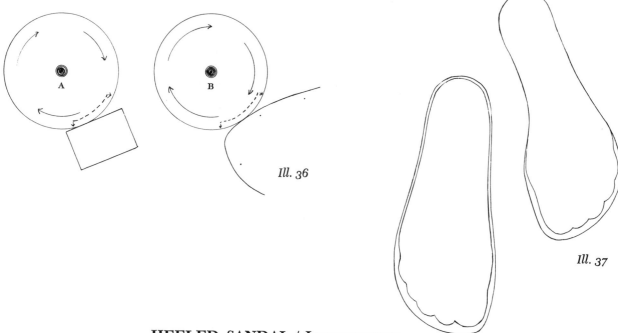

Ill. 36

Ill. 37

HEELED SANDAL / Intermediate

It is best to use an electric sander for these sandals. Don't attempt to make this pair (*Ill. 5*) or any other high-heeled sandals as your first project unless you are experienced with electric wheels and tools. This is essentially the same sandal as the flat sandal. However, because of the heel, it needs a metal arch, which is placed between the top and bottom soles.

Ill. 38

1. To make your pattern, stand on a piece of cardboard with your heels resting on a book or a couple of books built up to the height of the heel you want. (The cardboard is on top of the books.) Trace around your foot, being careful not to extend the heel or the instep area, but drawing 1/4″ extra around the toe section. (*Ill. 37*) If you have a pair of heeled sandals, take a look at them and see how the sole has been trimmed around the sides and back much closer to the foot than a flat-soled sandal would be. (*Ill. 38*)

2. Place your sole patterns *for each foot* on the leather and trace around them with an awl. Follow the instructions for the flat sandal to cut two top soles and two bottom soles. Wet the soles (*page 101*). As with the flat sandal, press the sole with your hands to shape it to the curves of your foot. But this time mold it to allow for the height of heel you want. While the sole is still damp, nail the arches in place (*Ill. 39*) with small tacks on the instep of the bottom sole.

3. Make your patterns (*page 98*) for:
   A. two toe straps 1″ wide and as long as is needed to go around your toe, through the top sole, and then meet underneath. (Mine were about 8″ long.)
   B. two arch straps 1″ wide and long enough so that each strap wraps around your foot, through the top sole, and overlaps at the side where the buckle is to be stitched.
   C. two heel straps, 1/2″ wide and long enough to go around your heel and attach to the arch strap.

4. Follow instructions for the previous sandal for fitting, cutting and finishing the straps. For this shoe, the top of the arch strap that overlaps should be tapered and skived so that it will fit into the buckle. (*Ill. 5*) The buckle is centered on the bottom part of the arch strap on the outer side of the foot. (*Ill. 5*)

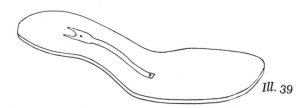

Ill. 39

5. As you did for the flat sandal, mark and punch holes in the soles for the straps. (*Ill. 40*) Put your toe straps through the proper holes, pulling them through with pliers if necessary. Your arch straps should be pulled through in the reverse way, that is, pull them through from the bottom of your top soles and out to the top. (*Ill. 41*) Attach the buckle by stitching around its center bar through the bottom part of the arch strap. The bottom strap should run under the top strap far enough for a continuous line. With a rotary punch, punch holes (*page 30*) in the trimmed edge the size of the buckle tongue. Attach the heel straps to the arch straps, riveting (*page 35*) or stitching in place.

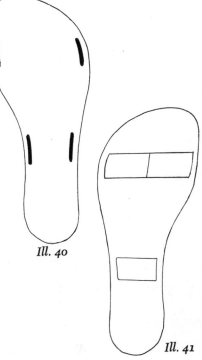

Ill. 40

Ill. 41

6. Cut a leather strip to fit over the metal arch on the bottom of the top sole. Glue this in place. (*Ill. 42*) Attach the toe straps as in the previous sandal.

7. Glue the bottom and top soles together in exactly the same way you did the previous sandal.

8. A stacked heel is best for your first pair of heeled sandals, but when you become more expert you can use any shape or height heel you like. You can buy heels with tops that are the size of the heel on your sole pattern or else slightly smaller. The edge of your sandals can also be sanded at an angle to fit the heels more exactly. (*Ill. 38*)

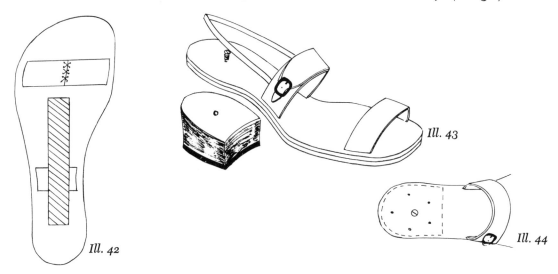

Ill. 43

Ill. 44

Ill. 42

To attach your heel, drill a hole through the center back of your sole and into the center of the heel, holding the heel firmly in its proper position. Screw the heel in place from the shoe down into the heel. (*Ill. 43*) When the heels are anchored, hammer in five nails around each screw (*Ill. 44*), angling the nails slightly toward the screw. If your heels are plastic, you may have trouble nailing into them. In that case, drill guide holes first with a small drill. If your heels need lifts on the bottom, place the heels on sole leather or rubber and trace around the heel. Cut the leather or rubber pieces out with a utility knife. Sand the nail and lift in place.

9. Cut a piece of top leather the shape of the top of your heel. Glue this on the top sole, covering the screw and the nails (*Ill. 44, dotted line*). You can also pad this piece of top leather with foam rubber or felt to make sure that your foot is protected from the screws.

THONG SANDAL / Easy

The soles of the thong sandal are made exactly like those of the flat sandal. Simply follow the directions for flat sandals to put together the soles, etc. The difference, of course, is in the thong.

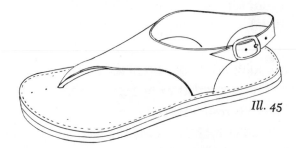

Ill. 45

1. Make your pattern (*page 98*) and tape it to the leather.
2. Cut the leather out along the lines of your pattern with scissors or a knife.
3. Punch two oblong holes at each side of the arch (*page 30*) and one round hole between your big toe and the next one. (*Ill. 46*)
4. Crease the thongs before putting them through the holes. (*Ill. 47*) This crease will make your toes feel much more comfortable than would a flat piece of leather.

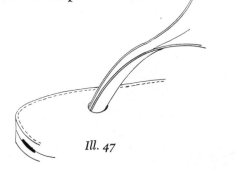

Ill. 47

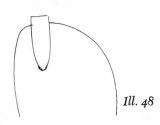

Ill. 48

Ill. 46

5. After you place the thong through the hole in the top sole, uncrease the leather of the thong and glue it flat against the underside of the top sole. (*Ill. 48*) The end of the thong should be long enough to run through the sole and out the toe. The extra is trimmed off after cobbling, but gives a visible guide for placement of clinching nails to go through the thong. (*Ill. 47*) Try to get at least two nails through the thongs as you cobble because they get a great deal of stress.
6. Attach the buckle (*page 38*).
7. Glue the bottom and top soles together and finish the sole edges.

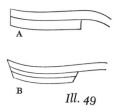

A

B *Ill. 49*

TO MAKE LOW HEELS

If you don't want a completely flat sandal, but prefer low heels, you can make your own. If you learn this technique, in fact, you can replace low heels on any of your shoes rather than taking them to the shoemaker. Place your sandals on sole leather and trace around the heel part of the sandal. Cut the leather to fit the heel. (*Ill. 49a*)

You can make a stacked heel by piling up several of these cut layers. (*Ill. 49b*) If your sandals are to be stitched by a shoemaker, don't add these heels to your sandal until after he has done his stitching, because he won't be able to get through three layers.

After stitching the soles together, glue the heel and as many layers as you like in place and cobble with heel nails. (*Ill. 50*) Sand and finish the edges of the heel as with the rest of the sole.

Never use both a heel and a leather arch. If you feel you need an arch, even with a heeled shoe, get yourself a metal one which is only slightly curved. Attach it as in the instructions for heeled sandals on page 109.

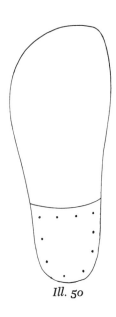

Ill. 50

Other Sandals

The following sandals are put together with the techniques you've already used in the basic flat, high-heeled and thong sandals.

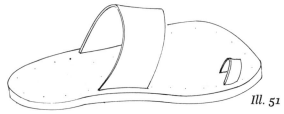

Ill. 51

TOE SANDAL / EASY

1. Make your soles as for the flat sandal.
2. Cut patterns (*page 98*) for:
   A. two arch straps 2″ wide and long enough to wrap around your foot, through the top sole to just meet underneath.
   B. two toe straps 1/2″ wide and long enough to go around your big toe and through the top sole, to meet underneath.

3. Tape the patterns to your leather and cut.

4. Attach the straps (*page 103*) and complete the sandal as in the flat sandal.

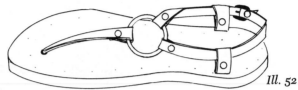

Ill. 52

RING SANDAL / INTERMEDIATE

The straps on this sandal are riveted around a brass ring.

1. Make your soles as for the flat sandal.

2. Prepare patterns (*page 98*) and cut the straps from your leather. The heel straps should be 1/2″ wide and long enough to go around your heel, with enough leeway to attach a buckle, and overlap around the brass ring, as in illustration 52. The thong also should be long enough to overlap the ring and extend through the thong hole, as in instructions for the Thong Sandal. Also note that the heel strap fasteners are made of one piece of leather, doubled and pulled up through an oblong hole made with the oblong punch in the sole to hold the ankle straps in place. These strap fasteners are glued to the underneath side of the top sole.

3. Attach the straps and buckle (*page 38*).

4. Rivets should be attached (*page 35*) where the straps overlap the rings and near the bottom of the heel fasteners to better anchor the ankle straps.

5. Complete as in the flat sandal.

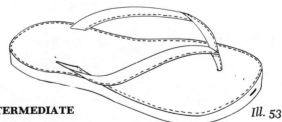

Ill. 53

THONG BATHING SANDAL / INTERMEDIATE

1. Make your soles as for the flat sandal.

2. Prepare pattern (*page 98*) and cut from the leather one strap for each foot. The strap should be 1 1/4″ wide and long enough (approximately 14″) to run from under the heel, around the foot, through the thong hole and out the front of the sole.

3. Fold the strap in half.

4. If you stitch the strap, pre-punch your holes (*page 29*) along the edge and stitch. Or just glue.

5. The two ends of the strap meet at the toe. Where they join, skive them (*page 27*) to make them less bulky, and stitch them together, as in illustration 53.

6. After the thong has gone through the top sole, it should be spread open as in the thong sandal, and clinching nails should be used to catch it.

7. Complete as in the flat sandal.

More Advanced Sandals

Now we are going to get into more complex sandals. I've given you very little information about them because by the time you're ready to try them, you should have a good deal of experience in sandal-making techniques. At this point, you'll be so expert that you can work from the drawings alone. Bear in mind that though sandal making takes long to describe, once you've made your first pair of sandals, you will be able to work easily on other designs.

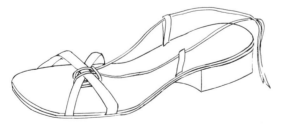 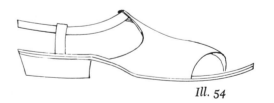

Ill. 54

NOVELTY SANDALS / Advanced

These two styles of sandals have straps which, like a sandwich, go between but not through holes punched in the soles. They are wrapped around the edge of the top sole at the front, though the heel straps and the thong (*Ill. 54*) go right through holes punched in the top soles, as in the earlier sandals.

1. Make your cardboard sole patterns for these sandals (*page 98*), but point your pen in slightly so that the pattern is cut very close to your feet, even at the toes. Cut out paper straps and fit them to your foot. Place them *under* the cardboard soles. They should look as though they come up from under your feet. Adjust the string ties.

2. Cut the straps out of soft leather, either suede or cabretta, with scissors. Cut out the top soles from cowhide about belt thickness and the bottom soles out of No. 5 or No. 6 iron sole leather.

3. Pad the top soles with foam rubber or felt right on the bottom of the top sole. Then cover the top sole and the foam rubber with suede or cabretta, drawing the suede down around to the underside of the sole. Glue the suede or cabretta in place around the edges of the top sole.

4. Punch holes with the oblong punch (*page 30*) to fit heel strap fasteners.

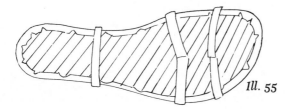

Ill. 55

5. Now fit the straps to your foot and put them in place. Draw them to the bottom of the top sole. Cement the straps in place. (*Ill.* 55) If the straps form ridges under the soles, pad them with felt or with scrap leather to fill out the space between each strap before putting the bottom sole in place.

Ill. 56

6. Attach heel strap fasteners (*page 109*).

7. Attach buckle (*page 38*) shown in illustration 56.

8. Cement the top and bottom soles together.

9. Attach the heels (*page 110*).

10. Finish the edges (*page 107*).

CROSSED OR BRAIDED SANDALS / Advanced

In these three sandals the leather is either crossed over or braided. The crossed sandal (*Ill. 57*) is cut from two straps which taper out toward the back and are fastened with a buckle.

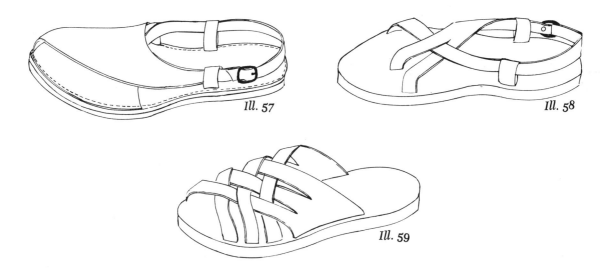

Ill. 57

Ill. 58

Ill. 59

The simpler braided sandal (*Ill. 58*) is made of two straps, with one strap slit in two, and the other pulled through it. Make sure that you don't slit all the way to the end of the leather and that the straps are long enough to go around your heel.

The more involved braided sandal (*Ill. 59*) has two wide straps slit in three for braiding.

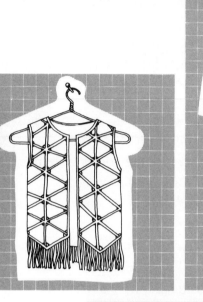

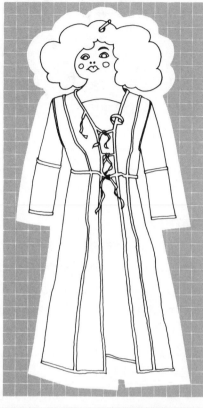

Garments

Making garments out of leather is as easy as making them out of fabric or other material. Almost any regular clothing pattern can be used, so I won't have to give you special ones in this book. However, do avoid patterns with too many seams, since they become bulky and uncomfortable to wear in leather. The same sewing techniques apply when working with leather as with fabric, except for those instances discussed below.

GETTING YOUR LEATHER

Decide what you want to make and choose your pattern. At the beginning it is best to use a simple pattern and to make your garment out of a lightweight suede, which will go through most sewing machines without trouble.

The pattern will tell you how much material you'll need in yards. Leather is bought in square feet, so you will have to convert the yards into square feet. For 54″ wide material multiply the number of yards needed by 13 and add to that 15 percent of the amount. For example, if the pattern calls for three yards of material, you will need 44 square feet. If the arithmetic is too much for you, ask for help in the store where you purchase your leather.

Buy all your leather at once. If you are making a pair of pants and think you might want a matching vest or jacket, buy enough leather for both pieces. Dye lots in leather, more than in fabric, vary, and if you decide on the vest later, chances are the color won't match exactly.

PREPARING YOUR PATTERN

Assemble all the pieces of the pattern. Check the measurements of the pattern against your body measurements, but be sure not to include the seam allowances when measuring your pattern. Make any adjustments in size that are necessary to ensure a comfortable fit. Don't attempt to make intricately fitted clothes of leather. Because permanent creases tend to form in leather garments at the elbows and at the knees, add 1″ to the length of the pattern for sleeves and legs.

Often the instructions for cutting will tell you to fold your material in half and place the pattern on the fold to cut your piece. Although this works fine with fabric, it can't be done with leather. The bulk in the fold will result in a piece bigger than needed.

What you have to do, then, is make a reverse copy of the pattern piece given as half a front or half a skirt, etc. Trace the pattern onto a large piece of paper, marking all darts, tucks, and seam allowances. Cut it out and tape the two pieces together, matching foldlines. (*Ill. 1*) Now the pattern is ready to lay out on your leather.

If your pattern has a square-cornered pocket, round the edges slightly. (*Ill. 2*) Square pockets, executed in leather, bulk at the corners.

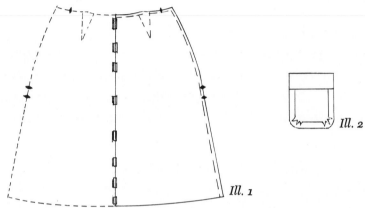

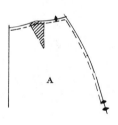

Ill. 2

Ill. 1

If your pattern has small darts at the waist and shoulder seams, it is often easier to eliminate these darts by actually cutting them out of the pattern (*Ill. 3a*), pulling the cut ends together and taping them closed. (*Ill. 3b*) It's all right if the paper pattern bunches a little. Suede or soft garment leather has the ability to mold itself to a contour, so your garment will lie flat.

If you're making something with a facing, like a vest or jumper, use a full lining (of a fabric, not leather) instead of just the pattern's facing pieces.

To interface (in a jacket, for instance) if your pattern doesn't extend the interfacing all the way to the armhole, do so yourself. It will help retain the shape of your top.

In lining a garment follow the pattern instructions exactly. Ask for help from your leather dealer in picking material for your lining. Usually a leather skirt or dress would need the same lightweight *fabric* as wool or other material would require to avoid rustle and bulk.

When you are using a new pattern, or if you are new to leathercraft, it is a good idea to make the garment in muslin to make sure it will fit properly, before actually executing it in leather. If your garment is to be lined, however, you can do this fitting with your lining pieces.

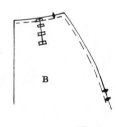

Ill. 3

Remember: you can take in leather seams, but you can't let them out, since they are cut, glued and punctured with stitching holes.

LAYING OUT THE PATTERN

Get out all your pattern pieces and all your leather pieces. Plan to use your best leather pieces on those parts of your garment that will show most (the front, sleeves, etc.).

Because suede has a nap, make sure all your leather pieces are running the same way.

Lay your pattern out on the top side of your leather. Tape it to your leather with strips of transparent tape about 3″ in length. Run the tape in lengthwise strips along the seam allowance. (*Ill. 4*) When you cut out your leather, leave the tape on the pattern to reinforce the edge.

CUTTING, MARKING AND BASTING YOUR PATTERN

Cut out the pieces with a good pair of scissors. When you come to a notch, instead of cutting inward, cut an outward triangle to indicate where the pattern pieces are to be joined. (*Ill. 5*)

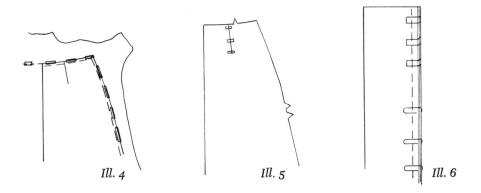

Ill. 4   *Ill. 5*   *Ill. 6*

On the wrong side of your leather, mark in chalk or pen any instructions from the pattern you might want to transfer—like darts, pockets. Also mark seam lines on this side, if you want a clearly visible guideline for your sewing (*page 29*). Remove the tape from any scraps of leather you wish to save. (If you keep the tape on the leather, it becomes gummy and leaves a dark spot when finally removed.)

After you cut and mark the leather, baste the pieces together, either with a basting stitch or by attaching the pieces of leather with paper clips or Scotch tape wrapped over the edges. (*Ill. 6*)

SEWING LEATHER WITH YOUR MACHINE

If you are using a sewing machine on lightweight leather, use a size 11 needle and thread it with polyester thread. For medium- and heavy-weight leathers, use a size 14 or 16 needle and heavy-duty cotton thread. However, if your machine offers a special triangular-point needle, use it.

Before you actually start sewing your garment together, use scraps of leather to experiment with the way your machine works on leather.

Set your machine at between seven to ten stitches per inch for leather. For lightweight suede, you can have as many as twelve stitches per inch, but be careful that these stitches aren't so close to each other that they perforate the suede and cause it to rip.

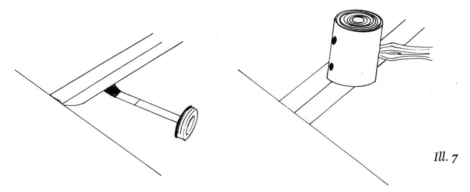

Ill. 7

If the leather doesn't move through the machine easily, put tissue or waxed paper under the leather and sew right through it. The tissue paper will allow the leather to slide over the teeth of the machine and can be peeled away from the leather after it is sewn.

PRESSING

Never put the iron directly on your work when pressing leather. Instead set the iron to "warm," put brown paper or a press cloth over the leather, and press lightly. Too much heat makes leather dry and brittle.

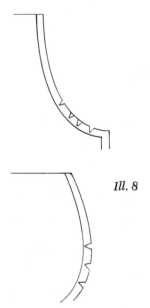

Ill. 8

SEAMS

Press all seams open. Then glue the seam edges down with rubber cement, tapping them in place with a rawhide mallet. (*Ill. 7*) If the seam curves, cut a few V's perpendicular to the seam, to allow some "give." (*Ill. 8*) Of course, don't cut too close to the stitching.

If you are afraid to put an iron to leather, simply press the seams open by hand and glue in place.

Decorating Your Seams: Seams can be topstitched for a decorative effect. When topstitching down both sides of a seam, make sure to start from the same direction on both sides to avoid a pull in different directions. (*Ill. 9*)

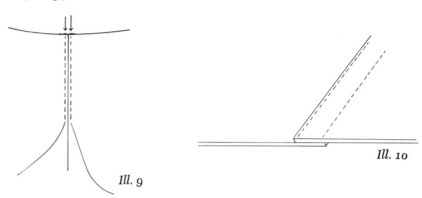

Ill. 9

Ill. 10

If you want a "jeans" effect on your seam, put one raw edge over the other and make two rows of topstitching, instead of turning the edges under. (*Ill. 10*)

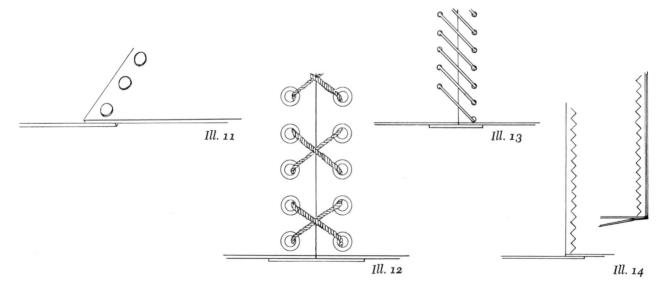

Ill. 11

Ill. 12

Ill. 13

Ill. 14

Instead of sewing the seam, you can rivet (*page 35*) it. (*Ill. 11*)
Or, put in grommets (*page 36*) and use lacing. (*Ill. 12*)
Or, punch holes and do a whipstitch (*page 33*). (*Ill. 13*)
Or use a zigzag stitch on a machine. (*Ill. 14*)

Or cord your seam by inserting a small covered cord into the wrong side of the seam and then turn it to the right side. (*Ill. 15*)

Sew your seam as usual and then decorate it with nailheads. (*Ill. 16*)

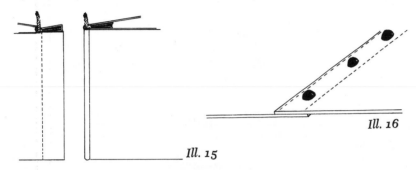

Ill. 16

Ill. 15

ZIPPERS AND BUTTONHOLES

Follow the instructions on the sewing pattern for zippers and buttonholes. On bound buttonholes, glue the facing to the back, rather than sewing it. (*Ill. 17*)

Ill. 17

HEMS

Hems in leatherwork are glued, not sewn. Mark hemlines in chalk or pen on the wrong side of your leather. Press all seams open (*page 121*). Put rubber cement all along the bottom of the hem and in a line on the inside of the garment where you want it attached. When the cement is tacky to the touch (*page 40*), tap with a rawhide mallet. (*Ill. 18*)

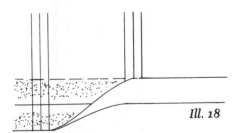

Ill. 18

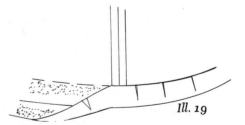

Ill. 19

When you have a circular hem, as in an A-line skirt, after folding the hem to the place you want it, cut a series of V's into the leather, making sure not to cut through the hemline. This will allow the hem to lie flat and will eliminate bulk. (*Ill. 19*) Make sure that all V's are glued down.

IDEAS FOR DECORATING YOUR GARMENTS

Make cutouts in your garment with an Exacto knife (*page 43*) and either leave them open or back them with contrasting leather or material. (*Ill. 20*)

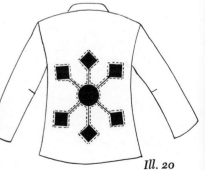

Ill. 20

Use contrasting leather trim on your garments (*Ills. 21 and 22*)
Make garments of patchwork leather or with patches of leather and
material. (*Ills. 23–25*)

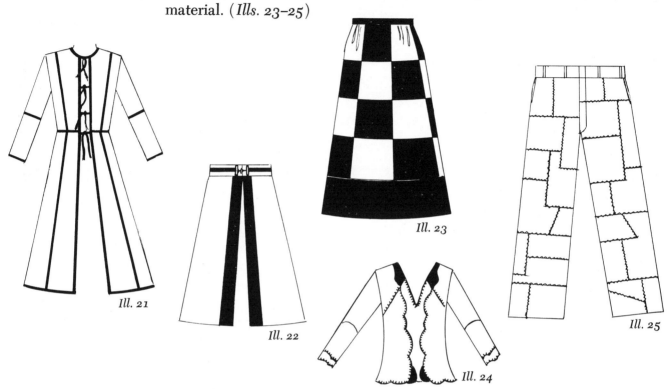

Ill. 21

Ill. 22

Ill. 23

Ill. 24

Ill. 25

Quilt your leather garment. (*Ills. 26 and 27*)
Cut out appliqués (*page 43*) of leather and sew or glue them to your
garment. (*Ills. 28 and 29*)
Rivet strips of leather together. (*Ill. 30*)

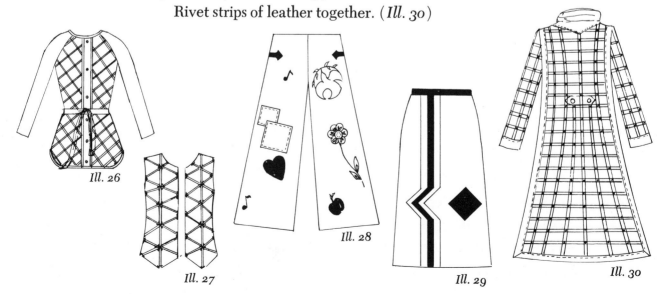

Ill. 26

Ill. 27

Ill. 28

Ill. 29

Ill. 30

HOW TO MAKE FRINGES

Fringe is a wonderful decoration for your garments. Some patterns for garments come with instructions for fringe and in such cases you should follow the accompanying directions. However, you can always add fringe to an article if you want to.

Take a piece of leather the width and length you want the fringe to be, plus at least 1/2″. Mark the back of it with cutting lines approximately 1/4″ apart. Then cut along the cutting lines with scissors to within 1/2″ of the edge.

APPLYING FRINGE

If you are making a jacket and want to add fringe down the sleeves, choose a pattern that has a seam running down the outside of the arm. Add 3″ to the pattern along the edge of the sleeve. (This could be shorter or longer, depending on the size fringe you want.) Mark these additional three inches of leather for fringe as above and cut to within 1/4″ of the seam line with your scissors. (*Ill. 31*) Then overlap the front fringe edge over the back seam of the sleeve and sew your sleeve together.

Ill. 31

When adding fringe to seams on pants, sleeves or dresses, it will eliminate bulk if you add the fringe between the seam allowances of both pieces and then stitch the seam. (*Ill. 32*)

If the fringe falls at the bottom of your garment, it is easiest to cut (or fringe) it without adding leather. However, if your leather is too short to fringe, take another piece of leather, fringe it and sew it to your garment by overlapping the wrong side of your leather to the right side of your fringe. (*Ill. 33*) Or simply turn the hem up and stitch the fringe to it. (*Ill. 34*)

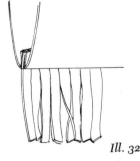

Ill. 32

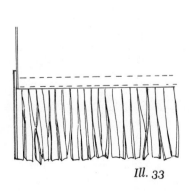

Ill. 33

Ill. 34

DIRECTORY OF SUPPLIERS

The following list of suppliers of leather and/or leather materials is meant to help you get started in leathercraft. It is by no means complete. You will find that these outlets will be of great service to you in fulfilling your needs or directing you to other outlets if they cannot do so.

For more local suppliers, consult the yellow pages of your phone directory under Leather Suppliers, Shoe Repair Suppliers, etc. Remember that many materials can be purchased in local hardware and craft shops.

If you still have difficulty getting supplies, write to the Tandy Leather Company, 330 Fifth Avenue, New York, New York 10001, for a catalogue and price list for mail order purposes, or for a list of retail stores across the nation (only a few of their 150 stores are listed below). A list of tanners can be obtained by writing the American Tanners Association, 411 Fifth Avenue, New York, New York 10016.

ALABAMA

Southern Leather Company
1125 Conception Street
Mobile 36602

ARIZONA

Southwestern Leather & Shoe Findings
27 North Third Street
Phoenix 85030

Tandy Leather Company
3925 East Broadway
Tucson 85711

ARKANSAS

Southern Leather Company
913 Main Street
Little Rock

CALIFORNIA

Fastener Supply Company
977 Howard Street
San Francisco 94103

Fastener Supply Company
319 E. Washington Blvd.
Los Angeles

MacPherson Leather Company
200 South Los Angeles Street
Los Angeles 90015

MacPherson Leather Company
730 Polk Street
San Francisco 94109

Sav-Mor Leather & Supply Company
1409 South Los Angeles Avenue
Los Angeles 90015

COLORADO

Colocraft Inc.
1310 South Broadway
Denver 80210

Tandy Leather Company
3977 Palmer Park Blvd.
Rustic Hills Plaza Shopping Center
Colorado Springs 80909

CONNECTICUT

New Haven Leather Company
254 State Street
New Haven 06510

DELAWARE

Tandy Leather Company
4389 Kirkwood Highway
Kirkwood Plaza
Wilmington 19808

DISTRICT OF COLUMBIA

Tandy Leather Company
712 Seventh Street, N.W.
Washington 20001

FLORIDA

Herzberg's Inc.
1213 North Central Avenue
Kissimmee 32741

American Leather Company
1609 Tampa Street
Tampa 33601

D. D. Holiday and Company
15 St. George Street
St. Augustine 32084

GEORGIA

J. H. Cook & Sons
200 Whitehall Street, S. W.
Atlanta 30303

HAWAII

Seafarer Leatherward Inc.
1409 S. Beretania
Honolulu 96814

IDAHO

Pioneer Company
Sixth and Main Streets
Boise 83701

ILLINOIS

Mandus Nelson & Company
564 West Adams Street
Chicago 60606

J. C. Larson Company, Inc.
7330 North Clark Street
Chicago 60626

Roberta Creative Leathers
296 Donlea
Barrington 60010

Lee Ward
840 North State
Elgin 60120

INDIANA

Schutz Bros.
North Manchester 46962

La Venta Corp.
R. R. 2
Box 103
Bloomington 47401

Pearson's Saddlery
2260 North Walnut
Muncie 47305

IOWA

Iowa Leather Company
Sioux City 51100

KANSAS

Roland Speh Leather Company
134 North St. Francis
Wichita 67202

Tandy Leather Company
7644 State Avenue
Wyandotte Plaza Shopping Center
Kansas City 66112

KENTUCKY

Geo. Bosler Leather Company
208 West Market
Louisville 40202

LOUISIANA

Southern Leather Company
118 Caddo Street
Shreveport 31102

The Southern Leather Company
950 Perdido Street
New Orleans 70112

MARYLAND

Arts & Crafts Materials Corp.
321 Park Avenue
Baltimore 21201

MASSACHUSETTS

M. Siegel Company
186 South Street
Boston 02111

Bergman Leather Company
103 South Street
Boston 02109

Ira Berman
147 South Street
Boston 02109

United Shoe Machinery
104 Federal Street
Boston 02109

D. B. Gurney Company
Whitman

MICHIGAN

Delco Craft Center Inc.
30081 Stephenson Highway
Madison Heights 48071

Tandy Leather Company
4823 Woodward
Detroit 48201

MINNESOTA

Gagers Handicraft
1024 Nicollet Avenue
Minneapolis 55403

MISSISSIPPI

Southern Leather Company
333 South Farish Street
Jackson

MISSOURI

Brown Leather Company
305 Virginia Avenue
Joplin 64801

Sam F. Tinnin
4014 Olive Street
St. Louis 63108

Konomo Distributor Company
108-10 East Missouri Avenue
Kansas City 64106

MONTANA

Montana Leather Company
124 South Main Street
Butte 59701

NEBRASKA

Lincoln Leather Company
822 "O" Street
Lincoln 68508

NEVADA

Tandy Leather Company
1235 East Sahara Avenue
Parkway Plaza Shopping Center
Las Vegas 89105

NEW HAMPSHIRE

Tandy Leather Company
20 Concord Street
Manchester 03101

NEW JERSEY

Patterson Bros.
45 Samworth Road
Clifton 07012

C. S. Osborne & Company
Harrison 07029

NEW MEXICO

Southwestern Leather & Shoe Findings
27 North Third Avenue
Phoenix

NEW YORK

Leathercrafter's Supply Company
25 Great Jones Street
New York City 10012

A. H. Standard Company
28-30 West 38th Street
New York City 10018

Martin M. Jordan Corp.
9 Murray Street
New York City 10017

Joseph Hart & Sons
16 Reade Street
New York City 10000

A. C. Products
422 Hudson Street
New York City 10001

Henry Westpfal & Company
4 East 32nd Street
New York City 10016

Craftsman's House
35 Browns Avenue
Scottsville 14546

D & L Leather & Supplies
427 Seneca Street
Utica 13502

Elton Leather Corp.
47-49 Spring Street
Gloversville 12078

NORTH CAROLINA

J. H. Cook & Sons
209 North Church Street
Durham 27701

J. H. Cook & Sons
122 East Liberty Street
Salisbury 28144

NORTH DAKOTA

Dacotah Leather Company
Grand Forks 58201

Tandy Leather Company
216 East Main Street
Bismarck 58501

OHIO

S & T Leather Company
333 East Long Street
Columbus 43215

Bailey Leather Company, Inc.
2212 North Fourth Street
Columbus 43215

Brodheat-Garrett Company
4560 East 71st Street
Cleveland 44105

Orrville Leather Company
228 Chestnut Street
Orrville 44667

OKLAHOMA

Bentley Gafford Company
14 West California Street
Oklahoma City 73102

OREGON

Oregon Leather Company
110 N. W. Second Avenue
Portland 97209

PENNSYLVANIA

Kline-Savidge Company
161 North Third Street
Philadelphia 19106

Tandy Leather Company
314 Blvd. of the Allies
Pittsburgh 15222

RHODE ISLAND

Craft Yarns of Rhode Island, Inc.
P.O. Box 385
Pawtucket 02862

SOUTH CAROLINA

Tandy Leather Company
2531 Main Street
Columbia 29201

SOUTH DAKOTA

Tandy Leather Company
513 Main Street
Rapid City 57701

TENNESSEE

Southern Saddlery Company
3001 Broad Street
Chattanooga 37402

Red Ranger Saddlery
1600 East 27th Street
Chattanooga 37407

TEXAS

Potts-Longhorn Leather Company
3141 Oak Grove
Dallas 75219

Tandy Leather Company
8117 Highway 80 West
Fort Worth 76116

UTAH

J. G. Read & Bros.
P.O. Box 469
Ogden 84402

VIRGINIA

Graves-Humphreys Inc.
1948 Franklin Road
Roanoke 24006

Richmond Leather Company
1839 West Broad Street
Richmond 23220

WASHINGTON

MacPherson Leather Company
1209 West Second Street
Seattle

WEST VIRGINIA

Tandy Leather Company
309 Washington Street, W.
Charleston 25302

WISCONSIN

Sax Arts & Crafts
318 East Chicago Street
Milwaukee 53202

WYOMING

Tandy Leather Company
229 East First Street
Casper 82601

CANADA

Capital Findings & Leather Ltd.
580 Kind Street, W.
Toronto 1, Ontario

Lewiscraft
284 King Street, W.
Toronto, Ontario

Interior Tent & Awning Ltd.
1340 Clark Drive
Vancouver, B. C.

Birt Saddlery
468 Main Street
Winnipeg, Manitoba

About the Author

PAT HILLS is an experienced craftswoman. She has worked extensively in leather, and the selection of designs in this book is only a small representation of her work. Mrs. Hills is also accomplished in the art of making jewelry and has taught both leathercraft and jewelry at The Kulicke Workshop in New York City. She and her husband now live in Mt. Vernon, Ohio, where they operate a craft store which sells their personally made leather objects and jewelry.